Contents

VOL 92 NO 4 WINTER 2002/

Poems

Essays

Reviews

The Questionnaire

Poet in the Gallery

Art

Poems

Michael Haslam

THE HIGH ROAD BROOM

and The Soft Dethroned

*

Startling Life, the starling glitter turns reflection from the sun
into an instant flock decision – quick and smart to stop and light
say on a tree wherever, voicing riot in their cheeks and lifting off
      together, surely, (swiftly, sweetly) as they please.

Witness, how a being's thought is like his being thought
      arising slowly as an heron from the heron shaw –
arose, a marvel not unusual, aloft.

An ousel from the bush restarts beguiling soft
      repeats.
Chaffinches wind each repetition, winching to a pitch.

The coruscating burden, spirit sprouts, –
a scene of earthlings would sound timber framed,
the water would drain from the heath.
The pieces pinched from common stock.
Entranced dales and values. Soft heart's
      declaration took the shape of this remark:
Who put the spirits of the season in the trees –
First answer: the same as put fire in the hearth.

We work. The radio repeats. What makes your face
before you wake – On second thoughts, not even angels visited before
the fell gush of raw living water. Earthlings. Only dying stops us
living things. The mysteriously religious hook on the spot in our tracks,
      where song, the step, must rise or drop.

*

The car was blown along the high road broom
Broom broom, the yellow broom.
                                        A black
smoke blew from chimney stacks, grew grey
in thinning airs and dissipates. Old fossil seams
        of fuel coal below.

Over the pass to drive, vacation gives
        permission to name divine, effloriance in life,
which reflection in consciousness promptly gives
through mirrors face and hat, the mountains of past behind.
Vast, pleasant, to rise from the brake in a flutter:
broom pods, seeds of besom, soon turn black and crack
        like a shot at game.

Over the hill. Keep it simple. When we pass the cross,
        then we have crossed the pass. The past.
Then scrub the wild fruit of a self-revealed variety,
too much entangled. Park up where you got to in the van.
Get out and look. Go further. Walk, A queachy herbage
underfoot. Some bunches of flowering rush. Not much.
The sheep drop pellets. A purple patch of vetch. The purslane,
pink, and herb-robert meet by the stream engage in verbiage
        while still they glaze the lilac hazel mist.

*

Some foolish trope was imposed as a crown
on the figure of thrones. My own
could have made a career. My settled chair
dates from the married days. The springs are gone
and the foam seat rests on a fitting chequer board.
The table is small, more stable, and a generation older.
It's here I sit and do compose
                            the fair kindred of ode, or
honey spoon and milk my oats into my beard
with so much spillage dribble –
        Each day is present as a plot of the weather,
days pass, a cloud of the brain,
        in the eye of the present weather.

Take this well-appreciated morning, being benign,
        (on the subject of thrones), fresh, glassesless
before a floriant myopia,
        I saw the figure on a delf-stone throne,
burning flute-stops for seasonal graces,
        the pastoral haunts of The Soft,
or counting pleasures: how many are soon
        done, bygone. Answer. First and Last. Love, only None.
Quite quiet too. Not one.

                            *

Park up and look. That
upland inn it does look closed. A plywood
boards the wind-holes, and a fireweed fills the yard.

Ragwort, Sowthistle, Mugwort
      Balsam and Dock,
their common interests themselves conspire
      in reclamation of the plot
that sees the last of some poor Soft
      straggle of Forget-me-not.

As it transpired it was decided
that I should forgo,
      and so I soon forwent
as one derided though
I landed in my native element.
      As matters go
of tax, farm, rent,
I do what is demanded.

*

On edge, high up, below some
castle of cold comfort, there's a mix
of mist and woodsmoke, driven drifts
              the worthless acres, barren
browned forest; potholed, patched tracks,
a scattering of solitary, dismal, almost feral dwellings,
              steadings, each one guarded by chained dogs,
and patrolled by office badgers.

Twixt spirits of the mineral heath
              and bituminous lakes, a tumult
breathing flares, intrinsic fitness, frolic and jape.

Look the great sump of our hearts is at sea
to the west, on the bright side of death,
a retirement coast, sort of droopy just
do as you please sort of tidal basin, ebbed.

                        There is
a chapel hollow where the chisel slid.

The soul, the spirit of the soft, almost a poet
shelters by appointment while the hangers-on
dig clay in the teeth of a January gale.

So wild a wind and loose the tether broke.
I work out in all weathers, squaring things,
              on several levels. Keep self in a calm,
and it sounds dumb but wish and toast,
as hit and taste,
              the casual holiness of un-named wells.

*

I was searching the wastes for the ghost
　　　of softness dethroned. Turned from the seat
of all regalia. A bow, a bowl
　　　of undistressed light, a Bowland Forest
Spectrum.

Fork for a king. One thought point ought.
The exercise is throne's vacation.
　　　　　　Broom turns stubborn. Furze of gorse
resumes. Summer zooms. Hay wakes. This afternoon
a brief but effective belief in quiescence
　　　overcame me in the stubble,
with the sunshine on the eyelids, as devotion basks
　　　in pre-religious glow.

The flower stands more wavering than stone, but no,
　　　the stone withstands more weathering. I could not myself
withstand a more glorious conquest. Softness reigned
　　　by generosity in some of the hardest country,
when down fell a figure to void for a roughcast spell,
　　　before fancy returns.

*

Where is Westmorland now? Where it was,
          there it is. And the Levels of Kent.
There they are, under water, moon and sun.
It looks like Eden.
It looks like Romany Common.
A scattering of fire in the waste.

Unmask the Face. We note the frowns
          of some Lancastrian asymmetry to come.
Divine Springs up The Lune.
          Around The Backbone. Equally The Spine.
You could make a cult of Rivers
          flowing out from Richmondshire, hunting
fairytale and pastoral with haunting doubt.
          That face is one of mine.

A spot at night somewhere in England isn't death
this time but a gap in the steps. This is not the top
but someone's personal tipping spot. I resist with some success
the notion that any of this could be pre-ordained. A gap.
          The Face Let Drop. A fire, a formula. Gone Out. A Trap.
Some kind of landing in the rain. An hearth of ashes' paste
          in the mouth of an old mine.

*

Come up from the coal-hole and
the past is all behind us now the future
stares us in the fire.
     The mind is such it could be thrown
with a bright wind, above the high-lit line –
remember valley moon, the space engulphed,
now earth bows low into a bowl
     of greenish mottled glow, vague deeps,
a shady page of sycamore acerbics –
little daylights know the golden saxifrage
     of as and where it grows.

Looking at flowers though we thought we had
been shed. What was poetic anyway about
the rose but thickly sentimental blood?
     The King is a Cunt in Some Accounts.

*

The past a home. The future fire. Cool draught. Coal shadow.
Cloaks and hooks. An alcove in the hall. The soul itself
sat on a settle by the clock, just when it struck
the very brass mechanics ringing on a single set of strokes
in monotone to open musical colloquium. I counted six.
The sound turns wrong, syruppy, wrong sticks.
I didn't know if they were angels or poetic figments –
a cream of salvation for burns while turning
         greenish in the gills and looking deathly sick. A token
of Love, that Bliss or something else when I was woken
by a knocking on the locked back door. But surely this
will be remembered as forever something more. And all
the drinking-halls and parlours'll be closed by then.

Writing in truth at home. I am truly through by light alone.
I do all this on paper with my pen,
         a glee of dizziness surrounding the priapics,
from the stove down in the parlour to the skylight in the attic
and bouts upon sheets between boards, happen gently
playing permutations of my prepositions before
proposing the selfhood, pure animal buck. I could only ask
the women if it must be so, in the bedroom between.
The wind winds up a pitch to white ear-foam.
         Nay let us doze.

And all that rhyme with those.
Nay let us patch my own.
I can be reached by telephone.

*

The swift fleet hope stayed incomplete,
the hope of staider float for breath,
and kiss flute whistles to the weather in the teeth.

A lad laid low. By law. A mudded fount.
Low brow, wrote white the snow with coal-
      black heather edges of a flat,
and tried it on piano,
      unsigned, of no date, no palm but wet
deserted waste
      beyond a door so long withstood
the weathering of the brain, just as
the virtuous chaffinch is bound to repeat,
      and the tup'll mount whenever.

The ring returns. Coughed up. Is thy bull able to pull
      a like abjection by the nose?
Spreading prickles on the boney heath.
The woody skirts beneath.
Fold field and farmyard ford.
And see each has a spring to its dwelling.
It's not dead, it's just the alternator's gone.
      The thing returns.

Stone Trough.
There Throned.
Unthroned.
The power lost. Look for a new one.

Mark Haddon

TRANSLATIONS OF HORACE

Odes I:iv

The warming west wind and the welcome change of spring unlock the grip of winter.
Windlasses haul dry keels down the beach.
The farmer and the flock no longer love the stable and the fire.
The meadow is no longer white with hoar-frost.

Cytherean Venus leads the dance beneath the overhanging moon,
and nymphs and modest graces
stamp the earth with alternating feet while blazing Vulcan
tours the heavy thunder-forges of the Cyclops.

It is time to weave green myrtle in your oiled hair,
or flowers growing from the softened earth,
time to sacrifice a kid to Faunus
in the shady forests, or a lamb if he prefers.

Grey death knocks equally at poor men's hovels
and at royal castles. Wealthy Sestius, the shortness of this life
prohibits us from setting out with great hope.
Nightfall, Pluto's shadow-palace and the ghosts you read about in poetry

will soon be at your heels, and then you won't be throwing knuckle-bones
to win the job of drinking-master at the feast,
or ogling the pretty Lycidas, who drives men wild
and will soon be making girls a little overheated.

Odes I:xi

Leuconoë, do not ask what ends the gods have given us
or scan your Babylonian horoscopes. This winter
wearing out the ocean on the pumice coast of Tuscany
may be our last, or Jupiter may give us more. We cannot know.
Accept what comes. Be sensible and pour the wine, for jealous time
is running even as we speak. Life is short. Cut back long hopes.
Don't trust in what's to come. Bring home your harvest now.

Anthony Caleshu

COLLABORATION: BETWEEN COUNTRIES

We were at the back of the back of the bus,
crossing from one country into the next.

Our jeans were dirty and more than fashionably ripped.
Up all night we planned on coming down all day.

He wore a small smile beneath his military moustache,
for which he told us he'd received numerous medals.

On the postcard, behind the Virgin Mary's veil,
he pulled a flake of hash flat as a thumbnail.

When we got back on the bus, everyone cheered. They were
unaccountably devoted to wild geese, and some had just flown overhead.

COLLABORATION: CLEANING UP THE PARK

I knew nothing about the underbellies of public places
Nor the private desires that were daily fulfilled there.

The pamphlet artistically depicted boys rough-housing
with language, and girls bent over backwards painting their toe-nails.

For four weeks I went in training, till I felt part of an
elite group, till I walked with a runner's high.

I imagined their moment of stunnedness, snapping
them back from the shadows they basked in.

My high horse was no match for their speedy recovery.
I begged for no damage, collateral or otherworldly.

COLLABORATION: MIGRATION PATTERNS

after *The Collector*

I am trying to make sense of this butterfly's flight.

After a night's driving, I am no closer than this small town that skirts my questions.

The townspeople keep dodging me with their shopping carts.

In this jam jar you can see I picked the cotton boll from a field near the airport.

I found the swallowtail drying his wings on a pasture's picket fence.

What we need now goes something like this:

The application of aloe on a sunburn, though not so physical.

I understand it is late, but I'll share with you everything I've gathered so far.

Carrie Etter

THE CULT OF THE EYE

Then I glanced over the treetops, the miles of pasture
the window shows me again and again,
and soon I began to believe the window;
I became a votary in the cult of the eye and the cult
of transparency, because after we spoke
I used a form of to be as an equal sign: you *were* transparent.
I gleefully forbore the skepticism of *seemed.*

Admittedly, I nearly said you *appeared* transparent,
but I put my ear to the window's mantra
and asseverated your sincerity without reserve.
If this is a love poem, that's because I'm ready to love everybody.
I'll gaze on the miles of pasture as the sun descends
and never think I must kneel in the dampening grass;
and you'll refrain, just for now, from remarking my naiveté.

Rebecca O'Connor

A BAG OF TANGERINES

About a dozen tangerines fell
out of my blue shopping bag
and rolled down the bus aisle.
That made them smile, though
it was only a bag of tangerines
rolling down the aisle.

A gentleman in a white tunic
handed me four at a time,
the lady next to me stooped down
and scooped up a few,
the bus driver slowed right down:
"Are they limes?" "No,
they're mandarins, tangerines –
a little bruised now."

STORM

. . . and if the wind should lift me
and bring me out to sea
I shall cast shadows
across your homeland
and your heart,
and scream with the wind, drowning
in the depths of the sea
that kept us apart,
drowning in the pool at Godmersham,
the Cork cove, under the cliffs
of the Bloody Foreland, the high rise car park
of the San Sebastian gravel and sands . . .

Mary O'Donnell

SUMMERHOUSE DREAM

Our first house is rented.
Mauve bedroom walls, thin curtains,
windows open while we make love in the daytime.
We joke about the bachelor next door,
his heavy footsteps on uncarpeted stairs,
the girlfriends we wish for him.
The kitchen sink is always blocked on Sundays,
when families visit. I long to forget
gravy and grease, to stroll
through the cornfield across the road,
be part of its yellowness.

*

In house number two, we learn
how dreams are spiked by mortgages.
I remember the predatory smiles
of jogging women, committee women,
experts in killer sports:
        the older ones
ease the balls off their men with every passing year,
slip them from the sac of innocent lust,
just by talking, talking. Some days I sweat,
frightened by the violent suburban silence
behind all the words.
Our walls offer no respite.

*

Later, I dreamed of a summerhouse, with octagonal walls,
a view of the sea. I tried to lay foundations.
It would be a place for making good
the snags, for rendering till smooth, for bedding down
before uncurtained windows.
Two shells curled together
on a gull's wing grey blanket.
Not even the ocean would part us.

Julian Stannard

LITTLE DREAMS

Nothing much happens here
though sometimes there's a drift of bodies.
Fabio who might or might not be gay
says *See you later, sometime, maybe!*
And there's this gem of a courtyard
if it weren't for that person still hanging there.
That's not true actually, I'm hallucinating.
I might have to tell the doctor about that.
And there are snatches of corridor with dust
which are leading to God knows where.
Sometimes she does, sometimes she doesn't.
The ceilings are vaulted, like little dreams.

ALBERGO DEI POVERI

Maude doodles over
from the *Albergo dei Poveri*,
takes St. Anna's Funicular
and arrives at a place
of tables and birdsong.
We kiss, kiss and kiss again.
Then Maude produces
a huge tin of biscuits.
'Your children must be starving', she says.
We order iced-coffee
and start on the biscuits.

Weeks later my children appear.
Tin moves in a wide circle.
Maude doodles back
to the *Albergo dei Poveri*.

Andrew Duncan

LES PAUL'S GARAGE STUDIO

On the dressing-table with the nail-paint,
Pfleumer's rolled gold skin that stayed
On tips of gold-lipped cigarettes
and never left a leaf of Pharaoh's smile.

Folding the sound, from the foil of scruples,
He sprayed a metal paste on plastic strip
And sold it to BASF for a
Minstrel cotton, a mint vortex.
From jeweller's wire
to suffusions of aniline dye
How small were the ripples
that laid the sand; how big were the
Blusters of musical smoke, from Ludwigshafen
And downstream.

Les Paul stripped the first Ampex that shipped
And added a fourth head
Turned, and walked straight into
Kiss of mirror halves of sound shell
Turned, and walked straight into
Brilliant cocoon from lacquer applique
Turned, and walked straight into
A stretch steady for four mint copies
Turned, and walked straight into
Wekausha, Wisconsin
By the river that runs both ways

Lost time that paints on loops
Aligned, looking down
On a ridge between two patterns,
Cutting silver away
To chase a picture on silver.
Butting sashes of fine shaved sound
A mask of narcissistic blond wood
With American-classic semiconductors pointing thataway
You put germanium together with Germany
That's when you've got
Purposeful distortions of the recorded groove

Linger o phantom as I retouch a mood
Flattering the
Dissipations of a simulacrum,
A dupe of time regained
A garage like that will never end

The Ampex Memphis pickup and fixit man
Says, That music won't stick to the tape
Because you haven't lubricated the tape

(Pfleumer invented recording tape; Les Paul invented double-tracking.)

MYTH INTO HISTORY

1. When myth becomes history

Breaking
the rim linking the story back to itself
A pipe broken at the end with Time flowing out of it
the arrival of character
the onset of calculation
Marble eaten by a fungus which takes its shape
Stone wings defiled by a web of pink blood
sound breaking up into words
Cheap prophets with rhyming oracles

from hymn to annal
The spattered windrows of the stars foretelling
the lairs of metals lagged in the earth
fall silent. From god-tale to chronicle
the divine responses set out as law-code
shimmering on the mouths of the courts, distracted into paradox

The count of limbs fixed
the son looking like the father
The birds who forget the language of men
The hills stop in their place
and the property boundaries are drawn to each other

The rain of objects corroded by symbols
striated by a pattern full of niches
where sense and meaning are twined together
its features recalling the symbolic
as damage, worked by adze, a speaking blade

A candid and sure-footed sound
so rich in partitions and symmetries
a group identity pouring over us without flowing away
a symbol that whirls the building around its head

hexagonal black temple of the tardy god
Calendar rites of reparative time
bathing in warm water with tamarisk, wax, pine-cones, oil and sugar
baraka transmitted from the dead
dish of flour saffron spikenard cloves & oil
the brain mimetic of star energies
the pattern lashed with interference shadows
breaking up at cellular level
a huff from the shaggy muzzle of a musk ox

2. On the margins of great civilisations

She sews what her mother sewed
the figures left from another age
disposed with the frontality of Parthian art
the ceremonial scene – justly recalled! –
signed with its objects
new linen sufficient for its realisation.
Attached with the tall hat or mitra, the akinakes –
It is Respendial, king of the Alans. It is Caspar of the Ardagarantes.
The royal insignia in likeness sufficient
for a lost observer. An embroidered towel
for peasant prestige, for the glory of huts
scutched linen stalks, dyed with the juices of plants

In the margins of the great empires
provincial cultures turning slowly on themselves
a self-locking aggregate crossing the rim
of recurring. The abiding, the filling. Tales
in the prison where Campanella was held

Occluded
at the place where nothing is altered, the bottom
of a great lake
Let us enter the greater forgetting
far from the decay of forms
mere laggards in the march of high ideas
make the likeness of goodness
make the likeness of companionship

In the fertile meadows, with the water-furrows
sacred objects of clay and bog-timber
the beer takes on the likeness of the birchwood bowl
outworn relics of ethnic migrations
Only what starts from zero is a game
only what is renewable is melody

3. *Anagoge,* or, When history becomes myth

Posed for the photographer
a reality that looks like the ideal
all gun barrels and hot black eyes
gazing steadfastly back, on the Campanian crag
paladin of regional apocalyptic lore
the brigand Luciana sewed up in leather pants
in apron, with folded cloth draped on head and neck
Mauser rifle and a brace of Belgian pistols for balance
wooden shoes and silver rowels
living on medlars, small birds, and chickpeas
a complete assemblage tilting the frame into myth

Swept away by the transformation scene
flesh all turned to wings
Luciana in linen
riding along the river Derwent on a winter afternoon
at one with rocks and water, drawing the sun down,
stars stitched to her shirt. A broad-brimmed hat.
Fulfilling the star cults of personal salvation;
the shining track, the elliptical ridings;
the sky catalogues on the charts at Gospel Oak.
Stars plucked from the tree that lattices the sun.

Sheenagh Pugh

TIMES LIKE PLACES

There are times like places: there is weather
the shape of moments. Dark afternoons
by a fire are Craster in the rain
and a pub they happened on, unlooked-for
and welcoming, while a North Sea gale
spat spume at the rattling windows.

And most August middays can take him
to the village in Sachsen-Anhalt,
its windows shuttered against the sun,
and a hen sleeping in the dusty road,
the day they picked cherries in a garden
so quiet, they could hear each other breathe.

Nor can he ever be on a ferry,
looking back at a boat's wake, and not think
of the still, glassy morning off the Hook,
when it dawned on him they didn't talk
in sentences any more: didn't need to,
each knowing what the other would say.

The worst was Aberdeen, when they walked
the length of Union Street not speaking,
choking up, glancing sideways at each other,
but never at the same time. Black cats
and windy bridges bring it all back,
eyes stinging. Yet even this memory

is dear to him, now that no place or weather
or time of day can happen to them both.
On clear winter nights, he scans the sky
for Orion's three-starred belt, remembering
whose arms warmed him, the cold night
he first saw it; who told him its name.

Brian Henry

A MAN, HIS DOG, AND SOME FISH

Lest we sink meaning through doubleness
or make the boat coast unduly west,
we'd better reel in all we've cast
and call it a morning, for morning's sake.

The gills on the slats make a noise
nothing like the water flanking us,
and the childish routine of demand-
shake-convulse is miles from our minds.

The way you lift your head, as if to yawn
into the cataracting day, would shake
the sternest beast to tears, or a moan
that reminds why one seeks, at last, the shore:

to sing, perhaps, against the surety
of the thing, to coax the water in.

John Tranter

WHERE THE BOYS ARE

after Callimachus, Epigram 42

Waking up, I'm half man, half headache
with half my soul dead or vanished,
or maybe gone to Florida, carried off
in a fever. Once, before the Age of Latex
and Heavy Petting, kisses were kisses,
not infections. Has my ninth life
gone again to amble, sunstruck,
where the boys are? But I begged them
not to give shelter to the runaway slave –
"Turn him out onto the street!" – *fat chance!* –
I'm searching here among the crowd of trash
in the back room behind the bar – won't you
help? He's here, somewhere, with the bad boys,
half a star looking for an answering flame,
hunting, restless, and ripe for death.

Robert Saxton

MIRROR WRITING

Bad licorice has got into one upper tooth,
a glancing knock with the rib of the scythe.
For destiny making things half right: a tithe.

My father's pointed out my mother's nurse
claims roots will often capture back their lease,
safe in the coastward footsteps of the Norse,

a scroll of salvage literate on a wreck.
Thanksgiving's in a tavern on the dock,
in an upstairs room: below is Ragnarok.

Anne Rouse

MOVE

It's risky to walk the streets in this state.
A bleached blond guy
holding hands with his boy love, tells me to MOVE.

I remonstrate.

I *am* moving, shadowed and thwarted
by the singular gravity of others.
(Cue for the screwing up of his face
in exasperated contempt.)

Well you may ask what brought this on.
Tonight it sings off me.
I'm bared to the pith, to the green quick.

Drunks, touts and scamsters
approach, to introduce themselves
on wet curbstones.

Simon Carnell

EARLY ROTELLA

As you emerge from the lit tunnel
    beneath the mountain
on the Passo della Cisa,
    in the oversteering Korean hire car,
night fallen conclusively meanwhile
    closes it shutter,
a galaxy of wiped flies
    on the windscreen.

Coloured paper,
    in flitters and pennons,
sticks out from the mesh on the back
    of the paper-mill truck in front,
reminding you of early
    Mimmo Rotella –
of "found" billboard posters,
    layered and torn,
to a matter of pure surface
    and texture.

Radio has news,
    of the G8 in Genova –
and this is what you'd seen:
    a stage-set, a jackboot, a Molotov,
serial photo opportunities.
    White highlights on the head
of bald Berlusconi.
    A fish-eye panorama of the harbour
and aquarium –
    in a brass button,
on a dress uniform.

ATTIC

The city's coming back to you a cut-up fold-in
of cities: all zigzag, palimpsest and switchback:
a cooling littered trail of scratched scratch cards
leading through it has to be a maze of brick

terraces to a stone-rose windowed and veluxed
attic beneath the stars, four walk-up flights up
in South Kensington. But there's washing hung across
the streets, so it can't be there – the attic's slipped

its moorings, your bolt-hole a boat, an itinerant eye.
Traffic till three in the morning, in earshot habituated
as to backwash in a seaside hotel, heard not heard,
and the comforting muffled rush of a distant railway.

Your taxi waits as wet flagstones doubling
the street's globe-lamps pool blurry other skies,
and the reading taxi driver's moment of inattention
lets you sidle, fixing him, along the wall and away . . .

Past four free-standing brick arches of aqueduct
or railway bridge; the steel-shuttered shopfront
of "Mr Boot"; the geological deposit or imprint
of a Roman arch jigsawed into a medieval wall stuck

with black-bordered fly-posted death notices.
Past the abattoir with its relief stone bulls' heads;
the pavement tree hung with a drying sheep's fleece;
the Victorian prison with its kitsch crenellated

turrets and air of something looming in Bavaria,
or lakeside in Berlin. Past the fake Tudor beamed
cottages dwarfed by upsprung high-rises, mirror-
walled, needling the air, maquettes in a dream

competition of lucid, future, rational architecture
(you the miniature stick figure included for scale) –
and past the Primitive Methodist converted chapel,
now a carpet warehouse. A burnt Cat earth mover

in a trash-strewn quarry. Quarry or building site?
A suburban run of out-of-synch traffic lights like
a flight of locks leads up to it; a small herd or flock
of sheep and goats night-grazing the forecourt

of a concrete block of flats; a low-riding finned
car motley with serial partial paint-jobs and rust
the only other thing moving, sounding as if repaired
with a hope, a prayer, and rideable lawn-mower parts.

The finned car has tracked you, it's your taxi and driver.
But you're back in your bolt-hole on the estate.
Or attic elsewhere? The city sleeps. One illuminated
lamp in the lamp shop. Back-lit curtains of an early riser.

Eve Kimber

LEAVING HOME

Long ago and far away,
where carrots wear pyjamas,
the were-wolves there wear flowered frocks
to wage war on piranhas.

My cousin dived into that world
riding a swimming dove;
my aunt swore I must fetch him home
to prove if I could love.

"Before his tea sets cold and hard
and leaves sprout from his cup,
go, fetch him home, and I'll believe
you have the devil's luck."

Because I was the quiet one
who did too well at school,
I mounted on a lemon shark
to prove I was a fool.

So long we swam, we dived so deep,
my breath was long since spent;
I swam on in a suit of bones
to where the sea-tides bent.

And there upon a tide of grass
my cousin, wreathed in flowers,
sat laughing with a lovely witch
who knotted up his hours

and tied them into daisy-chains
to bind his wandering feet.
I took him by his ring finger
and warned him of the heat.

"Your tea is getting cold", I said
"your Mother blows a storm,
if you give that witch your own fool's gold
I fear you'll come to harm."

He took me by my bony throat
and flung me in the sea;
he wrapped the witch in fool's gold chains
and followed after me.

And while he ate his tea at home
I lay beneath his feet;
he was his mother's hero still
and I, the stones of the street.

So up I rose a speaking stone
and went on my own way;
and whether I can love or not
is written in salt sea spray.

Clive Wilmer

BETHEL

When Jacob in the desert stopped
  For nightfall and the climbing stars,
He slept, a stone his pillow,
    Among volcanic scars.

He saw the angels of the Lord
  Ascending and descending there
In glory, with the Lord himself
    Above the topmost stair.

At break of day he set the stone
  An upright pillar on the ground.
It made the sky a heavenly roof
    And earth's foundation sound.

Jeremy Over

MUSEUM FOR MYSELF

For Peter Blake

Getting up, going out and talking to people are all part of it
one thing stuck to another from left to right
à nos victimes civiles et militaires
I will trawl around the toyshop
Typography

with the wrestlers
thoughts are things
as a little boy holding an image of himself as a man
as much as a brush is
bread   poultry   Ave Maria
a display of hats plays a crucial role
a sort of safety valve
Gayton Vicarage, Sonny Liston, hernia belts, student songbooks and dog food
acquired 1967

The extraordinary talents and generosity of Peter Blake
bits of wire and allusions to reproduction for Oxfam
a miracle visible in the work of the infinite
kinds of salami, an obituary cushion, the parents' bedroom,
Dumdie Doodles, the dissecting table and the umbrella Tuesday
introduced by fireworks so deftly
that the join is invisible   a tennis ball
painted to represent Ely Cathedral
or Dorothy
or a privet hedge questioning children
about, on the subject of, and approximately Eduardo
Paolozzi shaped like a battleship
every corner a great joy

So far so good
Everything is coming to an ordered conclusion
Knowledge was accumulated with care and difficulty to this end

No, I don't think so. No, not any more. No.
Not really.
It was. It could have been.
But I don't know. It depends.
Maybe in the past few years. Partly.
In a way, yes. Quite a bit. I think so.
Yes, Yes. I do, Yes.
Oh Yes.
Yes both.

THE WATERFALL ILLUSION

There was something (a smell?) in the hedgerow.
I don't know what but it was alive
and giving itself in the dark.
That and the confusion of folksong
head and shoulders above all the earlier influences
like slag heaps
and they surely will.
The virus is spreading like an inkstain
under foot and up the spine
the 'h' silent and inarticulate
as clouds in the weft and waft
of a fine caravan site in Annan
where we simply hurled our excrement over the hedge
to the Falls of Foyers where in 1834 Dr Addams discovered that if he stared for 20
seconds at a fixed point in the torrent, then transferred his gaze leftwards to the
adjacent rocky gully, the gully appeared to shoot skywards.

This is all going on in my trousers remember
eating cheese while St Jerome continues to read assiduously
in his study in the house on the lake although the lake is
merely suggested by an expanse of unrippled brass
and the island itself is no bigger than the house that sits upon it.

It's market day and now we know this everything changes.
An equestrian enters from the left, his horse playing the violin
extremely badly – even for a horse –
but it's music nevertheless for all occasions even this one
our necks twisting effortlessly as my father is born again
in the living room this year as in every previous year
and all our legs across the table
like it was midday
and there were no real people at all
only saints or tourists.
Who else would do this for you
in the middle of the *Adagio*
with your elbows for maximum effect?

Perhaps I should have said something else.
In one of the earlier drafts there was
a brass tap for one of the nipples
a toad in the plughole
the way her nose scrunches up
royalty on the patio
the official prunes.

Just lying in bed and thinking about it.
This is the best part.
I should like to preface my remarks by declaring a lifelong interest in the meat
and livestock industry.

. . . I long to see it.
. . . great Gibraltar, swift in Tirol, without knowing it.
. . . the belly and chin by ropes.
. . . and snow.

. . . ceilings.
. . . lately.
. . . prop the train, which is long and heavy when set on end.
. . . somewhat into its mouth.

. . . inquiry.
. . . mice, refusing the red.
. . . passage.
. . . raw with oil and pepper.
. . . in pursuit of the females.
. . . after an ineffectual search in Linneaus, Brisson, etc.
. . . gave it a ragged appearance.
. . . feet above the butt.
. . . in reality a bivalve.

. . . I am able to say.
. . . analogy.
. . . of roads.
. . . grass and leaves.
. . . and the larger bats.

. . . any advances.
. . . one indeed and found it full of spawn.
. . . a furlong or more.
. . . tables nearly digested.
. . . and laid up a good fund of materials for a future edition.

. . . the mere accident of finding the potatoes.
. . . or even the blue rag.
. . . enough is a circumstance still more strange and wonderful.
. . . safe and brisk in a glass decanter.
. . . cut for watering the meadows.
. . . in silence.
. . . on such a restless tribe.

AMERICAN EXPERIMENTAL MUSIC

Everything you can think of
all of the time
spread out in the hall

And at the other extreme
I am delighted to see
William and Mary

in and out of the piano
for hours at a time
during the breeding season

or pacing gingerly over the mud
in a piece called
Pacing Gingerly Over The Mud.

Alex Smith

ON A THEME OF APOLLINAIRE

The saints along the nave
and crucifix at the end
are veiled in their Lent purple.

Outside, a girl is sitting –
knees wide apart – on a bench
enjoying a lunch-hour smoke.

Her unbuttoned coat
is spread open, its lining
a purple sheen

in the spring sunlight.
She is almost
of the same religion.

Essays

The Poetry Review Essay

ROBERT POTTS

Apprehension

I'VE ALWAYS LOVED horror movies. We needn't forgive me for this: although those horror movies include, for example, Werner Herzog's *Nosferatu*, with its gorgeous, painterly Slovakian landscapes, or *The Beast with Five Fingers*, with Peter Lorre's splendid wheedling whispers ("I must have those books"), or tension-ratcheting Jamesian creepies like *The Others*, they also include many, many films that are, even by the standards of devotees of the genre, frankly appalling. Some are atrocious in quite the wrong way. Nonetheless, all are, in some way, instructive.

Take *The Texas Chainsaw Massacre* for example: a film that fell foul of the British Board of Film Classification (or Film Censorship as it was then known) during the "video nasties" furore in the 1980s. The film tells the story of five hapless youngsters who stumble upon a family of unemployed slaughterhouse workers who "have always been in meat", and who regard their visitors as potential food. The director of the BBFC, James Ferman, had two stabs, so to speak, at cutting the film to make it acceptable for release, but the film proved too slippery for him: because it relies less on obvious gore and more on "psychological torture", slicing out the graphic moments did nothing to diminish the peculiar horror of the film; in fact, it increased it.

In the 1980s, video (a briefly unregulated new medium) was seen as uniquely dangerous, in this case because it could penetrate the home with its potentially malign influence; so *The Texas Chainsaw Massacre* was banned under hastily created legislation. (The same panic now attaches itself to the Internet, and will give governments further opportunities to legislate. There is a moral, then, both in the film itself, and in the way it was treated: something about tools, and the various uses to which they can be put.)

The film is legally available now (people in the year 2002 being less corruptible than those of the 1980s and 1990s, presumably; or more plausibly because the once alien and monstrous has now become familiar and cosy), but for years I had a bootleg copy of the movie, bought in Camden market (and, weirdly, subtitled in Japanese). It did not turn me into an autophagous serial killer, nor a vegetarian, though it did remind me never to enter an abandoned house in the middle of nowhere, nor to "split up and go into the woods". The film is either very good or, for many people, strangely funny – the pantomimish aspects of horror tips easily into camp if not well handled, or if the audience is unforgiving. I wanted to see it primarily because I was not allowed to. As the BBFC had discovered, things can be more unsettling or demonic if they are hidden from view.

Critics, who generally make at least a pretence of rationality have particular difficulties when it comes to the emotive. Plato's anxieties about poetry "and her sister arts" – the fear of art's potentially corrupting and almost magical effect on an audience – are echoed in every subsequent censorship argument, to the present day; he'd have fitted in very nicely at the BBFC, for instance. Aristotle, the great taxonomist, offered us the more benign concept of catharsis, making art useful as a purgative. And Longinus grapples with the emotional effects of art in "On The Sublime". Whereas Longinus concentrates on establishing the points of style which might give rise to an emotional response – he offers, essentially, a model of rhetoric based on respect for past models and the maintenance of a proper "taste" – Edmund Burke, writing when Longinus's work was re-entering Western literary thought, reverses the approach: he tries to understand the emotional response by examining the style which causes it. His is an early blending of psychological and philosophical argument, an implicit reproof to the rationalising tendencies of the Enlightenment. It is a fraught argument, however, and its failures are as interesting as its successes.

Longinus wrote that "grandeur produces ecstasy rather than persuasion in the hearer; and the combination of wonder and astonishment always proves superior to the merely persuasive and pleasant", and "in literature, emotional and sublime features seem closer to the mind's eye". While he does attempt to define or classify this "ecstasy", it is by way of loosely associated examples. It is ironic that the final paragraph of the surviving and partial text begins with a quotation from Euripides – "it is best to leave such things at a guess" – before Longinus promises to "pass on to the next problem, that is, the emotions, about which I previously undertook to write in a separate treatise, for they seem to me to share a place in literature generally, and especially in the sublime...", at which point the MS terminates. (The same loss or lacuna occurs in Aristotle with regard to catharsis; as if classical texts mischievously repress any analysis of emotion in the arts.)

Burke defines the sublime as evoking fear and pity; "whatever is fitted in any sort to excite the ideas of pain and danger, that is to say, whatever is in any sort terrible, or is conversant about terrible objects, or operates in a manner analogous to terror, is a source of the sublime . . ." and argues that "when danger or pain press too nearly, they are incapable of giving any delight, and are simply terrible; but at certain distances, and with certain manifestations, they may be, and they are, delightful . . .". He thus places the sublime firmly in the field of emotional response and follows Aristotle in his belief that this is beneficial, cathartic, saying that "these emotions clear the parts".

Yet the bulk of his enquiry seeks a definition and explanation of the sublime beyond its utility, and beyond rationality. The attributes Burke grants to sublimity include obscurity, darkness, vacuity, and, above all, an absence of delineation. "To make anything very terrible," he writes, "obscurity seems in general to be necessary. When we know the full extent of any danger, when we can accustom our eyes to it, a great deal of the *apprehension* vanishes." Burke's thesis here, that knowledge or comprehension gradually negates the sublime is interesting; it implies, conversely, that the sublime is a threat to our structures of understanding. Apprehension, a taking hold of, a clear perception of, an understanding, carries with it an opposite meaning, that of incomprehension and fear. Burke uses the word in both senses in the course of his thesis.

The movement of "apprehension", as recorded in the *OED*, displays a spectrum between these opposite meanings. It means physical grip, or purchase; it means grasping with one's senses, perceiving rather than touching; it means grasping with one's mind – comprehension – rather than perceiving; it means sensing with one's mind, intuitively, rather than comprehending; and it means anticipating, expecting, predicting – generally fearfully. We have moved from a sure grasp to an anxious speculation. The word itself slips through our fingers, until it is hazy, indistinct. What started as physical possession has ended up as a haunting.

Burke's entire treatise, with its headings and sub-headings, its ostensible anatomising of his subject, is an effort to wrest under control the irrational side of art: that he is reduced to categorising the sublime as uncategorisable, that he cannot, by definition, rationalise a process that thwarts our rationalisations, is, I think, a warning to all critics: "That great chain of causes, which linking one to another even to the throne of God himself, can never be unravelled by any industry of ours. When we go but one step beyond the immediately sensible qualities of things, *we go out of our depth.* All we do after is but a faint struggle that shews *we are in an element that does not belong to us.*" (My italics.)

Consider Wordsworth:

> Power awakens the sublime either when it rouses us to a sympathetic energy & calls upon the mind to grasp at something towards which it can make approaches but which it is incapable of attaining — yet so that it participates force which is acting upon it; or 2dly, by producing a humiliation or prostration of the mind before some external agency which it presumes not to make an effort to participate, but is absorbed in the contemplation of the might in the external power, &, as far as it has any consciousness of itself, its grandeur subsists in the naked fact of being conscious of external Power at once awful & immeasurable.

Out of our depth and struggling; astonished; approaching without attaining; humbled, prostrate. These are moments of intellectual abjection which, while in some strange way pleasurable for the person experiencing them, are uncomfortable for the critic, whose authority lies precisely in rendering comprehensively intelligible the difficult matter before him. When Burke, and the Romantics, describe the material world in terms of the sublime, we are more comfortable. Vastness and vacuity are terrible we agree (as Pascal said: "the eternal silence of those infinite spaces terrifies me"); likewise we are able to grasp that smallness can also be sublime, as when Blake's "heaven in a grain of sand", accidentally anticipates the technologies that can show us the abundant extent of the microscopic (as in e. e. cummings's lines "electrons deify a razor blade / into a mountain range"). Literature frequently represents these sublime moments – it can describe their characteristics, for example, or the sense in the spectator of stunned astonishment. Wordsworth, in the *Prelude*, writes:

> . . . after I had seen
> That spectacle, for many days my brain
> Worked with a dim and undetermined sense
> Of unknown modes of being. In my thoughts
> There was a darkness — call it solitude
> Or blank desertion; no familiar shapes
> Of hourly objects, images or trees,
> Of sea or sky, no colours of green fields,
> But huge and mighty forms that do not live
> Like living men moved slowly through my mind
> By day, and were the trouble of my dreams.

Wordsworth's description of his troubled thoughts and dreams is a description of the processing of the new and overwhelming experience. Kant further develops the concept of the sublime, pointing to the role of the faculty of reason in bringing the overwhelming sensation if not into control, then at least into conceptual grasp; he describes (I paraphrase brutally) a shuttling between apprehension as awe or terror, and apprehension as comprehension: the making intelligible of an experience that swamps, dwarfs or stuns our minds.

Our critical reasoning sets limits on the vast unknown. But during the transition, our thoughts themselves are disturbed, led towards "unknown modes of being".

How much apprehension can we bear? As Edgar Wind remarks, in *Art and Anarchy,* "suspense is an awkward condition to live in, and we are persistently tempted to exchange it for some narrow but positive certainties; and yet we know very well that, as soon as the artistic imagination begins to work on us, we leave the safe shore for the open sea..." One notes how many of these responses use as metaphors the same geographical features that constitute the natural sublime: boundless seas; darkened, featureless and colourless landscapes; alien elements. I am tempted to make a link here between our reactions to art which unsettles and disturbs our categories, and our settlement of landscape; our use of walls, boundaries, borders, to protect what is familiar and exclude what is alien and threatening. In apprehension (as, again, horror movies show very well) there is a great deal of xenophobia. Paul Muldoon's collection *Hay* contains a punningly titled couplet called "Tract" which, in full, reads

> I cleared the trees about my cabin, all
> that came within range of a musket ball.

It is an image which Muldoon was contemplating as far back as the mid-1980s, when writing *Madoc,* and represents the action (and mentality) of those settling a country. Other boundaries emerge in the wake of settlement and conflict: the "peace walls" in Belfast, vast structures dividing sectarian communities, raised higher when the throwers of petrol bombs improved their aim and reach; the UN-patrolled "green line" between Greek and Turkish Cyprus; the "terror wall" built in the West Bank, costing £1m for every one of its 250 miles; the Berlin Wall, now torn into souvenirs; the new fortresses of luxury houses with private security, barred against god knows what; the holding centres at Dover and Calais; Camp X-Ray, beyond reach and beyond law. Muldoon's title links settled land with textual dogma: to grasp the pun does not mean we have grasped its full implication.

Poetry which represents and discusses apprehension is more common than poetry which creates it. In the conventional poetry of any age, it is our familiarity with the conventions that alleviates our apprehension. Take Auden's famous "September 1, 1939" as an example:

> I sit in one of the dives
> On Fifty-Second Street
> Uncertain and afraid
> As the clever hopes expire
> Of a low dishonest decade...

"September 1, 1939" has proved a resilient poem, much-anthologised, frequently cited: it quite understandably enjoyed another outing in the wake of September 11, 2001, and the various and agitated employments of it then were instructive, as were Auden's when he wrote it. It was strange to experience the poem freshly again; I realised that, as is the fate of good anthology poems, it had become so familiar to me that I was no longer reading it; it had become a consoling incantation, pure rhythm and sound bite, an accessory to my own apprehension.

It had done so, in fact, eleven years earlier, 1990-1, that bitter English winter when the

Gulf War was about to begin. The 1980s seemed to fit the bill nicely as "a low dishonest decade": just how dishonest was only to emerge fully in subsequent years, though the Iran-Contra affair in the US, with its catalogue of CIA-sponsored terrorism, gun-running and drug-dealing – and the impunity of its protagonists – had already been exposed, and then buried, along with a few of the witnesses; and in Britain, an "economic miracle" was ending with boarded-up shops in the high street, whole communities rendered workless, home-owners trapped in negative equity and facing repossession, and job insecurity a fact of life. My apprehension then – a fear of terrorism at home and catastrophe in the Middle East – is my apprehension now. Even the US President's name is the same.

To be satisfied with the fluency and rhetoric of "September 1, 1939", as I was then, is unwittingly to concur with the self-deceiving citizens it portrays that

> The lights must never go out,
> The music must always play,
> All the conventions conspire
> To make this fort assume
> The furniture of home;
> Lest we should see where we are,
> Lost in a haunted wood,
> Children afraid of the night
> Who have never been happy or good.

And indeed, Auden himself loathed "September 1, 1939"; he did not allow it to be reprinted in his lifetime. (When Lyndon B. Johnson hijacked the poem for a political advertisement in order to portray himself as a peacemaker, shortly before sending troops and bombers into Vietnam, it must have been the last straw, as Edward Mendelson argues.) Auden found the poem dishonest, its fine rhetoric over-riding what he believed to be the hopeless truth of a desperate situation. Nonetheless, the poem has become homely and familiar anyway, its music still playing decades later. It is a poem about apprehension that assuages apprehension. It is a poem about impotence which is written in masterful measures and with wholly successful rhetorical flourishes. It does not enact what it describes.

If poetry and art are anything more than placebos ("the lights must never go out, / the music must always play") I wonder what they might be. The "music" in Auden's poem is swing jazz played in that Fifty-Second Street dive. One thinks of Vienna waltzing, of Nero playing the fiddle. Of dancing in Bali. Someone recently wrote in the *Guardian* that "writers have agonized about the ability of fiction and poetry to cope with the enormity of [September 11]": and the question raised by that idle word "enormity" is interesting. The problem is not of scale , although the attacks were spectacular: I imagine that had we been shown the bombing of Afghanistan in close-up on every TV channel and from several angles, over and over, while hearing the last words of the citizens "regrettably" culled in those attacks, we might have found that "enormous" too. Rather, the problem is complexity: the threads of decision-making and economic interest that lie behind the apparently simple collection of TV images in which "innocent people" are killed by "madmen" and a "despotic regime" must be overthrown with "regrettable casualties".

Poetry that makes us properly apprehensive leaves us with no certain home; leaves us uncertain and having to think twice; makes us unsure if what we understand is what was in any way intended; leaves us searching for clues and contexts; challenges our assumptions about the world and about poetry: it stretches us, time and time again, to try, with no hope of success, to settle on the relationship between poetry and the world. To negotiate between response and responsibility. This perplexity, this suspense, is, perhaps, where thwarting the reader's grip is what in turn grips the reader; the poem apprehends the reader, rather than vice versa. Our rapacious desire to bring the poem within our existing boundaries contends with our surrender to the poem's new boundaries. I am reminded of an interview with the poet Trevor Joyce which I read recently:

> John Cage [speaks] of how he deals with the unexpected outcome of one of his "chance procedures", through which he discovers that he has produced a piece of music, a passage of writing, which truly surprises him, because he has allowed the processes to speak, and he must now respond to what they have said: "When I find myself at that point, in the position of someone who would change something – at that point I don't change it. I change myself. It's for that reason that I have said that instead of self-expression, I'm involved in self-alteration."

Into the Sacred Zone of *Lyubov* – Recent Women's Poetry from Russia

CATRIONA KELLY

WESTERN NEWS FROM post-Soviet Russia seems to come in only two kinds: bad, or non-existent. Mainstream coverage and feature articles make the place sound at once lurid and dismal: natural catastrophes and terrorist assaults, mafia gangs, gun sieges, a lively export market in human flesh, Northern industrial towns turning into ghost cities. Reportage about the arts has much the same tone, spotlighting, as it may, the collapse in standards at the Bolshoi, or the tribulations of orchestral musicians who have to survive on perpetual underpaid foreign tours.

It is all uncannily close to the kind of picture of life in the wild capitalist West that Soviet newpapers used to paint during the Cold War, and the level of accuracy is similar. The horrors chronicled are not imaginary (as I was writing this article, Russian special forces stormed a Moscow theatre captured by Chechen rebels, as a result of which over a hundred people died of gas inhalation). However, in reportage accidents and atrocities dominate in a way they don't in lived reality. There's no doubt that in Russia life often seems worryingly fragile, but defiance of adversity is as much in evidence as despair – as just a few minutes watching the traffic and pedestrians in an average street will make clear. The pervasive boredom and mildly depressive atmosphere of late-Soviet life have vanished, even if the predictability of Soviet existence has too.

Equally, while life is tough for many people working in the arts, post-Soviet life is not just more stable than is supposed, but a good deal more vibrant than in the past. Journalists may suffer the occasional crackdown from political leaders who object to frank reporting about the Chechen conflict, or are riled when their behaviour is criticised too frankly (or even worse, openly mocked). But artists enjoy pretty well complete freedom of speech (for just about the first time in Russian history). And the collapse in state subsidies hasn't affected literature nearly as badly as it has labour-intensive arts such as cinema or theatre. Big journals may be less secure, but smaller ones have sprung up in large numbers. Opportunities for publishing poetry, in particular, have significantly improved over the last decade. Not only do general literary journals (especially *Znamya* at the moment) continue to publish good new work, but since 1994 there has been an outstanding Moscow magazine, *Arion*, entirely dedicated to poetry, essays, and reviews: a worthy successor, in terms of production values and editorial policy, to the literary journals of the early twentieth century, such as Valery Bryusov's *Vesy* (The Scales).

Certainly, literature no longer enjoys the automatic ascendancy it had during Soviet power. Soviet censorship constricted talent, but also sheltered serious writing from competition. During the post-Soviet era, on the other hand, commercial writing started to flood the marketplace. By the mid-1990s, the circulation figures of literary magazines had collapsed, and a significant section of what Soviet commentators liked to call "the most avid reading public in the world" was avidly reading astrology pamphlets and detective novels. Even career intellectuals, such as university academics, had less time for literature, since most now had to work far longer hours (often in several jobs) in order to earn enough to survive. But the result has been a kind of "normalisation" according to which literature is now produced, and read, by people who really care. German tea-sets and videos may have replaced hardback books as trophy objects in the display cabinets of the fashionable, but the many excellent bookshops of major Russian cities are always crowded, and the materials on display are far more varied than they would have been even ten years ago.

Russian poetry, which traditionally thrives on thin air, is doing well in the exacting new environment: women's poetry perhaps particularly so. Not since the 1920s has there been such sheer energy and variety in the work being produced. Journal editors recognise the vitality of the new tradition that is growing up. While Aleksei Alekhin, the editor of Arion, has announced that "divisions according to gender should apply only to changing-rooms and public toilets", he also estimates that about half the new poems he prints are by women. Much women's work also appears on the many internet sites dedicated to Russian poetry, and a search with, say, google.ru will also turn up intelligent and engaged critical literature, not to speak of interviews and other pieces airing the views of writers themselves.

On turning to the work itself, one is first of all struck by the confidence and individuality of the many young women now writing. It's become customary to describe the main tendency as "baroque", but the term doesn't fit. Flip, sardonic, self-consciously urban, this work is very much of its own time, and has more in common with Anglophone poetry of the last few decades than it does with the traditional Russian "feminine text".

A kind of quicksand ran underneath Russian women's poetry for the first two centuries of its existence. Poetry was the genre in which women came to prominence in the late eighteenth century, when women first emerged as writers; poetry was also the genre in which Russian women made international reputations – every serious reader of poetry in the West has heard of Akhmatova and Tsvetaeva, at least. Poetry is also the genre in which Russian women have written their greatest masterpieces: Akhmatova's *Poem without a Hero* or Tsvetaeva's *Poem of the End*, or the lyric poems of Karolina Pavlova, Zinaida Gippius, Anna Prismanova, Mariya Shkapskaya, Vera Merkureva, Bella Akhmadulina, and Elena Shvarts, to mingle famous names with personal favourites.

Yet many of the women who produced poetry of great authority were also tormented by the notion that what they were doing was somehow bizarre, freakish even. The sense of this is caught in two poems written by Akhmatova. The first is a humorous epigram in which she rebuked the many women who had followed her example by putting pen to paper: "Could Dante's Bice write as well as he / Or Petrarch's Laura sing the songs of love? / I was it who taught women how to speak, / But God, who'll stop their mouths?" While this denies the "crowning privilege" only to other women, another, more private and considered piece, undated but probably also dating from Akhmatova's last years, expressed anxiety about even Akhmatova's own place in poetic tradition:

> So, though I cannot take my flight
> out of the flock of swans,
> this truth, alas! I must admit,
> all poets must be men.
> If not, the world turns upside down
> till death brings final parting:
> a park's no park, a house no house,
> a meeting not a meeting.[1]

The heroine of *Swan Lake*, Akhmatova's implied referent here, is held beyond human nature, condemned to the inevitability of separation and death, by an internal flaw rather than by a magician's spell. The upside-down world that she inhabits is not the acrobatically inverted, easily rightable universe of the carnival: it is eternally out of kilter. The oddity of the situation is fully absorbed by Akhmatova herself: the last four lines express not just the strangeness, for a woman, of writing any poetry, but the strangeness, for a woman, of writing the kind of poetry that had made Akhmatova famous: verses of brief encounters and vexed separations in St Petersburg parks and domestic interiors.

Traditionally, the Russian woman poet was constricted by two enduring suppositions. The first – as in other countries – was the Romantic supposition that genius must be masculine. This meant that women were faced with the choice of identifying themselves primarily as "women" (and hence creators of a secondary order), or as "poets" (and hence not female). Tsvetaeva's narrative poem *On the Red Horse*, for instance, spurned female gentility (as Tsvetaeva considered it) in favour of explicitly masculine *genii*. Akhmatova, alongside her lamentations on the uncanniness of the woman poet's role, confidently located herself in the male tradition of Dante and Pushkin.

Whether or not they chose to write "as women", poets came up against the second supposition: that there were two mutually exclusive types of female creative mind. A product of the neo-classical tradition that dominated Russian poetry through from the late eighteenth century to the late twentieth, this supposition contrasted the sensual versus the cerebral, self-immolating and frigidly reserved – in terms of legendary classical poet-types, Sappho and Corinna. In generation after generation – Karolina Pavlova versus Evdokiya Rostopchina in the 1840s, Akhmatova versus Tsvetaeva in the 1920s, Akhmadulina versus Moritts in the 1970s, and Elena Shvarts versus Olga Sedakova in the 1980s – this ancient formula floated to the surface.

During the last ten years, though, these old ideas seem to have vanished from view, or nearly so. Now, if they are invoked, the tone is often ironic. It's surely no accident that it's precisely Akhmatova's biography that one poet now in her twenties, Polina Barskova, chose

---

1. All translations are by Catriona Kelly, unless otherwise indicated.

to burlesque in her "Evening at Tsarskoe Selo". A tryst between Akhmatova and her admirer Nikolai Nedobrovo misfires, but not for the conventional Akhmatovian reason of the man's failure to realise what a prize his companion's love is. Rather, at fault is the lyric heroine's own shifting mood: "He wants to know! She doesn't want. [...] / And then, dear God, she bursts out laughing / and night sneaks up and licks their shoes" [2]

Refreshing, indeed, is the sheer amount of laughter – and laughter as a sign of joy – in new work. There was always a light verse tradition in Russian poetry, but from the Romantic era on it was kept strictly corralled, turning up at ritual events such as the *kapustniki*, or holiday parties in institutes and theatres, when light-hearted rhymed mockery of workmates and work routines was the order of the day. (More dangerously, a Moscow acquaintance of mine managed to turn the entire content of a Brezhnev speech into rhyming couplets when attending one of the compulsory monthly "socio-political discussion sessions" at her place of work in 1981; this got her the sack.) In the early twenty-first century, humour can even make its way into the sacred zone of "*lyubov*", love-making, previously seen as the place for effusion of sentiment at all costs. (There's a famous anecdote about a Russian woman who said on one of the first live Soviet-American television discussions to be broadcast in the late 1980s, "There is no sex in the Soviet Union". What she actually meant was that Russian intimate relations were not mechanical, commercialised, and calculating in the way that the term "sex" suggested. This, while no more plausible than the idea that Soviet citizens were somehow able to do without copulation, at least honestly captured a widespread view of what "love" ideally ought to be like.)

Now, from Vera Pavlova, for instance, we have a totally different view of "love": knowing, self-aware, and by previous standards brazen:

> I'm in love, but not up to my ears.
> Waist-high only. Above that, conscience rules.
> So, take your palm off my breast, much desired though you are
> By my infernal lower half.

Pavlova's poems don't always seem as assured as this. They're sometimes so etiolated, so devoid of figurative language, and so relentlessly teleological that they work rather like computer print-outs of a body strapped to laboratory electrodes in order to monitor orgasmic sensations. (One is reminded of Nikolai Nikolaevich, the gormless hero of a novella by Yuz Aleshkovsky, paid to masturbate in a laboratory as part of an experiment, and climaxing to sounds of a loudspeaker voice announcing "Attention! An orgasm is occurring!"). But as antidotes to the familiar poison of love agony, even electronic orgasms have their uses.

Sacrilege with regard to previously sacred subjects isn't the only novel trend. Younger women poets also address topics that by Russian conventional tastes are scandalously unpoetic. The topping on a pizza, say (in a poem by Marina Kildibekova), or computer disks and beer-drinking: Darya Sukhovei's "Spring Scales" has the haunting melancholy of a modem's start-up song:

> with a new mouse and two books
> in a semitransparent polyethylene
> bag

---

2. Translated by Peter France

with dreams like a refrain

take the trolleybus take the trolleybus

what for what for[3]

Consolingly for those of us who have reached an age where we like to believe that turning forty doesn't mean a disastrous ebb in creative powers, the last two to three years haven't just been remarkable for the emergence of brilliant twenty-year-olds. Some established poets have also produced better work over the last few years than they have for decades. One case in point is Elena Shvarts, who emerged as a brilliant and vivid talent in the 1970s and 1980s, but seemed to be treading water for a while in the 1990s. Two recent collections show how she has been pushed by the death of her mother into an astonishing state of raw, yet argumentative and rational, pain. Witness, how, in *The Savage Script of Recent Times*:

> I'm bored to death being separate.
> Let me dissolve like a fizzing aspirin in water.
> I'll slough off my absurd two-legged skin,
> and be everywhere and nowhere at once,
>
> everything and no-one, at any rate not one of the many,
> these rubbed fragments, crumbs of mandragora.
> I don't want to fly down artificial hills
> like a child on a toboggan, braking with my heels.
>
> I will not peer through these green slits in my skull dome
> and make love with the air through the holes in my nose.
> On this carousel of fire I won't spin and spin,
> the sunset catching my nape, my mouth scorched by the dawn.

Bella Akhmadulina has also recently lived through a crisis (in this case a brain operation) to rally in an artistic as well as personal sense. Her work since has included meditations on her own condition, a fine elegy for the murdered St Petersburg politican Galina Starovoitova, and "Emplotment" (from her volume *Serendipity*), a piece in which she contemplates her own life. Akhmadulina was born in 1937, which, as no Russian reader would need to be told, marked the centenary of Pushkin's birth as well as the height of the Great Purges:

> This infant, born in thirty-seven
> not gifted more with prescience
> than any child, hadn't a notion
> the chime of dates was a life-sentence.
> For hadn't half the world been widowed,
> for hadn't half the world been killed,
> when newspapers and books brayed on:
> "A Century Since Pushkin's Duel"?

---

3. Translated by Christopher Mattison

This infant, born in solitary,
had hardly opened blue-grey eyes
inside its cot, when someone hurried
to report its birth to the police.

The rest of the poem goes on to evoke a "model childhood" like a Soviet version of Christa Wolf's. Yet at the same time, the references to school textbook stories about the sufferings of children in the capitalist world, or to Pioneer and Komsomol marches, are paraded in a style which constantly echoes Pushkin's dignified and detached mature work.

In English, however, Akhmadulina's poem raises a whole set of problems to do with taste and translatability. Once the central literary association is stripped away, little is left of the original except for cultural phenomena that don't exist in the Western world – if rendered into English, the complete poem would probably have to appear in an aureole of footnotes. Likewise, there's a poem by Tatiana Shcherbina whose lyric heroine ponders on eternity while using a telephone in a *podyezd*, the often stinking, much spat-upon and copulated-in, gangway into a block of flats. Translations such as "lobby" or "entrance hall" would make the situation sound much too *Brief Encounter*-ish, when it depends on a contrast between the degradation of the setting and the metaphysical aspirations of the speaker.

The difficulties of words that are "cultural spaces" rather than rigorously defined concepts beset prose translation, too, of course. More specific to poetry (not just women's) is the pervasiveness of direct and hidden citation. Paying veiled or direct homage to one's predecessors (or conversely, echoing some phrase of theirs in contempt) has been one of the most important practices in serious Russian poetry throughout the twentieth century and into the twenty-first. The practice marks a major difference between this and late twentieth-century Anglophone poetry, which has recently been passing through a phase of what the Russian critic Yury Tynyanov called *novatorstvo*, or determination to cast off the past. In Russia, closeness to inherited tradition is (usually if not always) seen as a mark of subtlety, not of insularity or incapacity to adapt. In a poem beginning "Distance is stretched out like a sail" for example, Svetlana Kekova clearly echoes the elevated locutions found in the sententious yet elusive philosophical poetry of Pushkin's contemporary Fyodor Tyutchev (1803–1873): "For inasmuch as we must slide / along a skin above the brink, / we will not injure God's wide world / with sadness that brings no reward".

More accessible for Anglophone readers are probably the poems presenting humble post-Soviet genre scenes. These are not just chronicles of daily life, but allegories of personal crisis. For instance, Shcherbina manages to turn the disappearance of hot water in summertime Moscow (a yearly summer nuisance in all Russian cities) into a meditation on personal loss, pain, and physical disintegration:

They've cut off my hot water,
love's juice, the verbal flow.
I'd like to complain to the nation,
but they'll shut me up too, long before.
Without moisture, I'll dry out,
along with the dirty dishes and the washing.
I'll get mouldy, gather moss,
I may even graduate to long-forgotten![4]

And Tatiana Voltskaya's very direct, demystified vision of winter is at the same time satisfyingly elusive, shifting perspective with a Pasternakian sleight of hand:

> Snow grows old, like an actor you knew as a child,
> It sags like a drape, so that footsteps keep on escaping
> The dim mirror of the wind – you're happy, alive or dead –
> It's not important, flushed or pale, – here's a make-up artist,
> Surging upwards, tracing cheekbones with a powder-puff.
>
> Suddenly you're somebody that nobody knows.
> Alone on this evening, your every movement will
> Dissolve in an instant, without reflection.
> Snow falls outside the frame, dark beckons with a nod,
> And you lie, curled up, along the edge of the bed.
>
> Without a reflection in somebody, you are without being.
> Deaf, and mute, and unseen. Crows' nests are swaying.
> The wheel has rolled past, its tracks are silvery scars,
> The heavens have torn apart – their edges billowing,
> And the moon drifts past in a wide, frozen halo.[5]

Any metaphysical domain appears at the interstices of perception here, and the division between perceived and imperceptible worlds is not easily binary in the way that it has traditionally been in Russian poetry since Symbolism.

Women's poetry at the moment seems to have broken free of any "female tradition" as previously understood. This has not, though, brought with it assimilation to poetry written by men. One can hear echoes of Brodsky in the approximate rhymes of Tatiana Shcherbina and in her clashing intonations, where borrowings from foreign languages jostle archaisms; but in terms of substance, Shcherbina is doing something new. Internationally, too, this is a tradition that's going its own way, partly because there isn't an easy way for Russian women to absorb Western women's poetry. Prose and cultural theory are being widely translated for *New Literary Review* and other journals, but few snatches of foreign verse see the light of day. What has resulted is a poetry not easy to classify in terms of international developments, but which is intelligent, challenging and above all individual.

---

4. Translated by Daniel Weissbort
5. Translated by Emily Hardiment

Suggestions for further reading:
History and Criticism Adele Barker and Jehanne Gheith (eds.), *A History of Women's Writing in Russia* (Cambridge, 2002); Barbara Heldt, *Terrible Perfection: Women in Russian Literature* (Bloomington, 1987); Catriona Kelly, *A History of Russian Women's Writing, 1820-1992* (Oxford, 1994); Catriona Kelly, *Russian Literature: A Very Short Introduction* (Oxford, 2001); Catriona Kelly and Stephen Lovell (eds.), *Russian Literature, Modernism, and the Visual Arts* (Cambridge, 2000); Marina Ledkovsky, Charlotte Rosenthal, and Mary Zirin (eds.), *Dictionary of Russian Women Writers* (Greenwood, Conn., 1994); Stephanie Sandler (ed.), *Rereading Russian Poetry* (New Haven, 1999).
Anthologies Catriona Kelly (ed.), *An Anthology of Russian Women's Writing, 1777-1992* (Oxford, 1994); *Modern Poetry in Translation* no. 20 (2002), "Russian Women Poets", ed. Valentina Polukhina; Christine Tomei (ed.), *Russian Women Writers* (2 vols., New York, 1999).

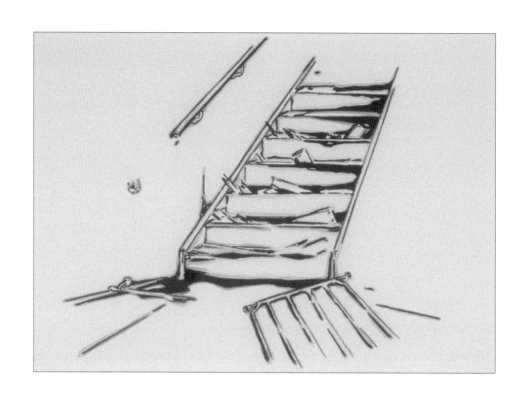

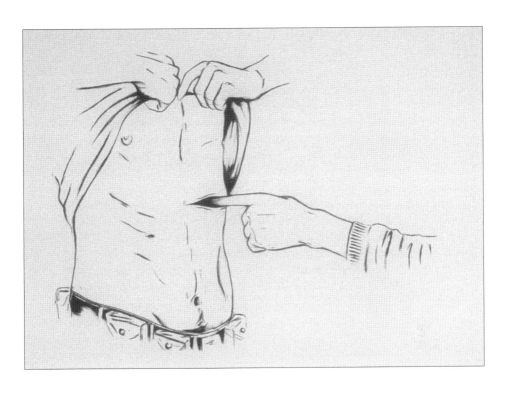

Redneck Kid Grows up on Farm

STEPHEN BURT

"I HAVE FOUND the world / so marvelous", A. R. Ammons once declared, "that nothing would surprise me". Many poets make it distressingly hard to find the best way into their work. Reading A. R. Ammons, on the other hand, you can begin almost anywhere and find, at most a marvel, at least a surprise: which is especially lucky since his vast *oeuvre* offers so many places to start. Ammons, who died last year at age 75, won almost every award an American poet can win, among them the National Book Award, the Bollingen Prize, a Macarthur "genius" grant, and the rare "award" of having his U.S. publisher, W. W. Norton, keep all his works in print. His volumes of verse, laid end to end, would easily exceed 1500 pages: *Collected Poems 1951-71* tops 350, while his last book of short poems, *Brink Road* (1996), and his last long poem, *Glare* (1997) together occupy over 500.

The pleasures of reading Ammons cannot be separated from the procedures and the personality which produced so very, very much work. Ammons was not a fox but a hedgehog, exploring the same large truths and the same winsome or homely tones over and over. And yet the one general thing his poetry knew, and kept explaining, grew from his attention to specialized – often, to scientific – points of view. These points of view, in turn, led him to emphasize the littleness of everything we can know: Ammons sought and found humility, flux, provisional order, and homeostasis wherever he looked - in the human mind and in the body, in forests and rivers, on Earth and in space.

He explored these preoccupations in a broad array of free verse forms. A palm-width (but fairly thick) 1991 volume offered *The Really Short Poems of A. R. Ammons*, several as short, and as permanently memorable, as "Small Song":

> The reeds give
> way to the
>
> wind and give
> the wind away

Then there are his really long poems. Ammons' first book-length work, *Tape for the Turn of the Year*, took its name from the roll of narrow adding-machine tape on which he wrote it over a few months in 1963-64. It aspired to include all the thoughts Ammons entertained while writing it, plus anything else a reader happened to bring in: the poem asked, early on,

> who
> are you?
> can I help? is there any
> thing I can do:
> are things
> working out
> all right for you? what
> are those black areas?
> are they parts
> of you that can't

> fall into place,
>   come into light?

Later book-length poems included 1974's *Sphere: The Form of a Motion; The Snow Poems*, a 1977 verse-diary; the consistently self-deprecating, usually funny, unusually wise *Garbage* (1993); and its semi-sequel, *Glare*.

Ammons also wrote lyric and essayistic poems at more ordinary lengths. Until the early 1970s some of those poems identified their author with Old Testament, or even Sumerian, prophets, carrying words to the skies and the winds' high places. (Sometimes the skies or the winds replied.) Ammons' other characteristic modes remained with him throughout his five decades of writing. One such mode makes whole poems from natural scenes:

> The ice-bound spruce boughs
> point downward
> as if to
> slide their sheathes off

Another mode ties poems together from strings of "sayings":

>   people are
> losing propositions: what
> they build flakes away,
>
> even when they don't
> take it with them:[…]
>
> a worm cores this world's doings, look out.

In several-page "walk poems" and verse-essays like "Corsons Inlet", these modes of saying and seeing interacted as Ammons described his thoughts while passing uphill, round a lake, or down the road.

Those modes found raw materials in Ammons' life. The poet grew up on a farm in North Carolina where (he later wrote) "the only book we had at home was the Bible". Poems drawn from his childhood remember horses, mules, pine woods, and two younger brothers who died in infancy; "I saw his coffin being made", Ammons has written of one, "and I watched as he was taken away, his coffin astraddle the open rumble seat of a Model A". *Snow Poems* included a capsule autobiography:

> Redneck Kid Grows Up On
> Farm Goes Through Depression
> But Thanks to Being In
> Big War Goes To College
> Gets Big Job Making
> Big Money
>   (relatively speaking)…
> MAKE NO MONEY
> BUT
> WRITE NICE
> (tries hard)

Ammons entered Wake Forest University on the G. I. Bill as a pre-med, and left with a bachelor of science degree and a spouse, Phyllis (who survives him). During the early 1950s he served as principal of an elementary school on Cape Hatteras, then pursued graduate study in English at the University of California-Berkeley (where the poet-critic Josephine Miles encouraged him). From 1952-61 Ammons worked for a biological glass company in New Jersey; there he wrote most of *Ommateum*, with *Doxology* (1955), printed by vanity publishers in Philadelphia. *Expressions of Sea Level* (1961) began his rise to prominence; the mid-1960s brought a job at Cornell University, in hilly, snowy Ithaca, N.Y., along with several more volumes of short poems. Those books together made him a much-admired poet by the early 1970s, when Harold Bloom (a friend from Cornell) joined other critics in championing his verse. Ammons remained in Ithaca for most of the rest of his life, observing "snow / sifty as fog" and "ice's bruise-glimmer"; the lakes, heights and heavy weather of upstate New York informed his later poems as North Carolina informed his earliest.

Most young poets assimilate many styles before they discover their own; Ammons instead learned a lot from a few. From the Old Testament he took the elevated sense of vocation which he first imitated, then reversed. From Wordsworth he took his devotion to nature and solitude, and the idea that (in Ammons' words) "A Poem is A Walk". From Whitman he took the idea of a poem and a line as extensions of personality, able to "reach out broadly across the page in space-hungry gesture". Finally, in William Carlos Williams Ammons found most of his technical tools: irregular lines and thin-sliced stanzas; a variable, enjambment-dependent cadence; and the idea that a short poem can mimic, or equal, a reed, stream-bed or tree. (A somewhat later influence was Ralph Waldo Emerson, whom Ammons claimed he read on advice from Bloom: Emersonian concepts and attitudes color most of his longer poems.) "I've written most of my poetry more or less in isolation", Ammons once said, and his *oeuvre* remained at a great distance from the schools and movements which dominated much U.S. poetry during his lifetime.

Ammons' most important backgrounds were neither literary nor regional but scientific. "Most of my study was in the sciences", he told one interviewer. Helen Vendler once explained that Ammons' work "speak[s] from the processes of science"; he "habitually thinks of the world in scientific terms, and sees us very much at the edge of the galaxy, and by no means at the center of the universe". The natural sciences' methods and attitudes (in other words) do much of the work for Ammons that religious, cultural, political, or art-historical models do for other poets; Ammons takes advantage both of the hard sciences' perspectives, and of their unusual verbal properties. After a windy night

> I thought, my word, icicles
> summarize the rate of melt
> and wind direction, are a glacio-spiral
> version of a wind-rose: nature
> that will uproot an eavesload
> of history
> can be so careful of history

The mid-1960s series "Guitar Recitativos" keep one eye on youth culture's breathless lusts, and the other on Ammon's own, chemical models; the results are deliberately, irreproducibly, comic:

Baby, there are times when the mixture becomes immiscible
and other times we get so stirred up I can't tell
whether I'm you or me
and then I have this fear of a surprising reaction in which
we both turn into something else

powdery or gaseous or slightly metallic

Whether he's trying for laughs or for ontology, Ammons' attention to his own thought goes hand in hand with his attention to the non-thinking, non-speaking, non-human objects and scenes he so liked to contemplate. "If people (cruel / and insensitive, survival pluses) ail / you nature is a rescue, go to it", *Snow Poems* declared. For all his chattiness, Ammons often seemed more comfortable with the sciences' non-human world than with society, preferring forests' or galaxies' systems to ours. In consequence Ammons both liked, and understood, the idea of nonteleological, nonhierarchical, hidden (and only apparently random) order. One early poem comes close to installing chance as God, complete with Urim and Thummim:

My dice are crystal inlaid with gold
and possess
        spatial symmetry
about their centers and
mechanical symmetry and
        are of uniform density
and all surfaces have equal
coefficients of friction for

my dice are not loaded
        Thy will be done

If the young Ammons found religious tropes attractive, the older poet found that he neither needed, nor wanted, "celestial guidance systems". Ammons' beliefs, as they inform his verse, grew at once from a democratic temperament and from a scientific worldview (indeed, they argue that the two are linked). Like Whitman, Ammons went out of his way to exalt the lowly, not through any Christian program but as part of the spirit of inquiry: one poem invites us to

Honor the maggot,
    supreme catalyst:
he spurs the rate of change:
(all scavengers are honorable: I love them
all,
will scribble hard as I can for them)

Ammons' attraction to non-human systems, his understanding of forms we find but do not make, also made him a poet of ecology: "in an enclosure like earth's there's no place to dump stuff off". Ammons titled his most ambitious (and most nearly political) long poem *Sphere* partly because it imagined the Earth seen from space, and partly because the "sphere" in the astronauts' photos offered Ammons an alternative to older, "pyramidal hierarchies" in representing knowledge or life as wholes. No poet has ever been more alert to the ways in which the material world resists our desires and our plans. Yet Ammons saw, and preferred to stress, not the gaps between ourselves and clouds or lichens, but the continuities – we are, as they are, homeostatic systems: "Honor a going thing," he wrote in "Mechanism", "goldfinch, corporation, tree / morality: any working order, / animate or inanimate".

Ammons saw his own poems as "going things," too. *Brink Road* defined poems as "Evasive Actions"; as "swerving (lessening and/ swelling) elongations"; as "connecting misses"; as "reminder[s] not of keeping but of not keeping". In *Lake Effect Country* (1983) poems were "Dismantlings", "Measuring Points", ways to "let / the quibble speak". His prose claims that "poetry resembles other actions such as ice-skating or football", and that "writing poetry is like surfing . . . If we miss or if the wave isn't right or fulfilling – that is, if the wave is not a whole motion of unfolding, an integrated action – we spill". Yet any spill, Ammons realized, could itself fit into a large enough "whole motion"; he learned to take into his orderly actions, or unities, all manner of random, by-the-way discoveries of "multiplicity" (his term). The much-anthologized "Corsons Inlet" celebrates just such self-revising incorporations of error and mess:

> I see narrow orders, limited tightness, but will
> not run to that easy victory:
> still around the looser, wider forces work:
> I will try
> to fasten into order enlarging grasps of disorder, widening
> scope, but enjoying the freedom that
> Scope eludes my grasp, that there is no finality of vision,
> that I have perceived nothing completely,
> that tomorrow a new walk is a new walk.

A poet who viewed all poems as "action and // action's pleasure", all things as processes, all particles (in a conscious echo of quantum theory) as waves, Ammons liked turning nouns into verbs, and *vice versa*: in the late, careful "Minutial Impress", "is" means "being" and "being" means becoming – "even the / biggest is, returning, plays out through / history extraordinary ragged changes". As critics have started to notice, Ammons' poems about fluctuating systems can also evoke the "extreme dependence on initial conditions" which came to define chaos theory. The older disciplines of cybernetics and systems theory, which view all patterns as patterns of information (and which developed early enough for the young Ammons to assimilate them) explain some of these striking coincidences, which let him celebrate, at once, the forms he found and the chaos they failed to contain.

Ammons' smaller-scale formal choices grow from the same open ongoingness that dictates his poems' overall shapes. He tends to alternate details with abstractions, as if to illustrate the interdependence he likes to invoke: "the exception sharply noticed / becomes the groundwork / of the next familiar". Rejecting most devices (rhyme, for instance) which set poems apart from prose, Ammons favors the rhetorical figures poems can share with other speech, especially chiasmus ("poison earth, eat poison"). His aural arrangements rely on tone and phrase-based rhythms, rather than on any intricate euphony; they emphasize interdependences and apparently-improvised movement, rather than attempting pre-set shapes. Ammons also depicts his beloved complexities by keeping lines and arguments in overlapping motion, never allowing one aspect of form (a metre, a syntactic figure) to control all the others. Even Ammons' peculiar punctuation gets into this self-revising, ongoing act. Sometimes he eschews punctuation entirely. Usually, though, he simply avoids full stops, or uses just one (at the end of the poem): everywhere else, he uses not "." but ":" The colon itself comes to stand for his attitude, since it is (as he is) never conclusive, always moving on, ever ready to introduce a new topic, or a list, or a ratio.

Ammons' antihierarchical informality also governed his whimsical choice of topics. *The Snow Poems* comprehends American football, ecology, weather, farts, weather, sex, cooking, grief, wit, and weather, weather, weather. *Sphere* included "the autopsy and the worm", "an isoceles triangle", "a piece of pie", "dandelion, protozoan, bushmaster and ladybird", hydrology, sexuality, elegy, "desk chair, wheel-back side chair", "glassware, software and willow ware", all within 100 lines. Ammons' diction also advertises his inclusive outlook: he especially likes the extremely abstract, and the colloquial or scatological, registers most poets avoid:

> lucky for the pheasant they
> have a big ass and long
> tail to sustain them above the
> snow when their legs blop through

Ammons' last poetic accomplishment seems to some readers his most personal and most moving: his sense of himself as a physical, natural body, and his sense of himself as finally inconsequential, made him a great poet of old age. Near the beginning of *Garbage* Ammons considered adopting a frugal diet based on soybeans ("more protein by weight than meat"): what else would a poet in retirement need?

> Social Security can provide
> the beans, soys enough: my house, paid for for
>
> twenty years, is paid for: my young'un
> is raised: nothing one can pay cash for seems
>
> very valuable

One late short poem decided that "Teeth are distressing only/ if you try to save them". Another, "A Part for the Whole," exercised its synecdoche on Ammons' feet, their "arches bone-sprung crack flat":

> feet, good feet,
> don't leave me up here with
> the one place to go
> and no way to keep from going.

Against such quiet or folksy lines, we might set serious passages like this from *Sphere*: "I expect to die in terror: / my mother did: old songs (hymns) erupted from her dying / imagination: they say she sang them blurred for two nights".

Even before he wrote his poems of old age, Ammons' cosmic contexts let him become a major poet of *memento mori*, even of *contemptus mundi*; "earth, no heavier / with me here, will be no / lighter when I'm gone". He liked, and meant, both his declarations of wonder, and his statements of resignation, his lowerings and modifications of once-salient prophetic ambitions. His poems frequently compare (or contrast) lives to seconds, hours to aeons, geological and cosmic to quotidian time. Many of his strongest passages remind us how little we mean, how little we do, how much we fail to see: they tell us, in other words, how to react to the inhumanity of nature's laws, the fact that the real ground rules of our time on earth come neither from us, nor for us:

> when we learn we are trash
> flimsy, flowable, our holding
> trivial and slight, we must
> not say, if that's what
> the universe thinks of us, so
> much for the universe:
> it should be the benefit of our
> experience here to realize trash
> the just groundwork
> of marvelous devising

Though Ammons has had imitators (and talented students) he has exerted little stylistic influence on younger poets: his inventions have proven inseparable from his peculiar (and charming) way of seeing the world. Ammons' greatest achievements arise in his longer poems – partly because the long poems are simply more original (their closest precedents remain distant indeed), partly because in the shorter poems, though many of them turned out very fine, Ammons' sense of the poem as "saying", as action, could keep him from loading every rift with ore. (The lesser short poems, and there are many, tend to end cute: "drinking this sweet rain, consuming this green".) Of the many self-explanations his poetry offers, my favorite may well be "The Put Down Come On", whose sixteen lines encompass both his humility and his wonder, his scientific predilections and his characteristic light touch:

> You would think I'd be a specialist in
> contemporary literature: novels, short stories, books of poetry,
> my friends write many of them: I don't read much
> and some drinks are too strong for me: my empty-headed
>
> contemplation is still where the ideas of permanence
> and transience fuse in a single body: ice, for example,
> or a leaf: green pushes white up the slope: a maple
> leaf gets the wobbles in a light wind and comes loose
>
> half-ready: where what has always happened and what
> has never happened before seem for an instant reconciled:
> that takes up most of my time and keeps me uninformed:
> but the slope, after maybe a thousand years, may spill
>
> and the ice have a very different look withdrawing into
> the lofts of cold: only a little of that kind of
> thinking flashes through: but turning the permanent also
> into the transient takes up all the time that's left.

A shorter version of this essay appeared in the United States in *Ruminator Review 9* (spring 2002).

Reviews

Twists and Turns

EDNA LONGLEY

Paul Muldoon, *Moy Sand and Gravel*
Faber, £14.99, ISBN 0571215351

IS THE TITLE of Paul Muldoon's new collection a tease, an irony? One of his "pawls and pranks" to quote *Madoc*? Or has Muldoon's poetry always been more racy of the Irish soil than its postmodernist pigeon-holing allows? Perhaps those who read Muldoon (like Joyce) as a flux of floating signifiers presume that Ireland is one too. This is the case only up to a cultural and political point: a point sometimes missed by Anglo-American constructions of modernism as well as postmodernism. The linguistic self-consciousness of Irish writers has a context in epistemologically volatile conditions. Indeed, Muldoon's title refers not only to the thing itself but to its processing. "Moy Sand and Gravel", as the title-poem reveals, was a Co. Armagh firm which washed "what had flowed / or been dredged from the Blackwater's bed", and then "wash[ed] it again load by load, / as if washing might make it clean".

The symbol implies Muldoon's own Augean labour of linguistic hygiene. In this collection his deconstructive drive reaches Auschwitz without forgetting the problematics of "Moy". These problematics make local specificity a principle of structure rather than of content. Muldoon's effects are at once precise, provisional and mysterious. His beautiful "Cradle-Song for Asher" epitomises a whole aesthetic:

> When they cut your birth cord yesterday
> it was I who drifted away.
>
> Now I hear your name (in Hebrew, "blest")
> as yet another release of ballast
>
> and see, beyond your wicker
> gondola, camp-fires, cities, whole continents flicker.

Muldoon refreshes words by seeing how far, like his son's name, they will travel. "Unapproved Road", commissioned for a book about the Irish border, centres, or decentres, on an encounter in Rotterdam between an Irish Republican speaker and a nomadic Tuareg whose "disregard" for frontiers cuts two ways. The poem offers alternative translations of the place-name *Scairbh na gCaorach* (rampart of rams / crossing of ewes); rhymes *Scairbh* with zarf (an oriental coffee-cup-holder); and ends with a parable based on the device of parison – corresponding structure in a sequence of clauses:

> "It had always been my sense," I hear him still, "that the goat fades into the goad
> and the spur fades into the flank
> and the fastness fades into no fixed abode ..."

"Goat"/"goad" is not just word-play or textual flux. The assonantal, associative "drift" of Muldoon's poetry keeps history in its sights. Word fading into word is an aesthetic that might dramatise either possibility (*Scairbh*, zarf) or conflict (goat, goad). Elision exposes oxymoron. One approved road not taken by Muldoon is any way of thinking that ignores cross-fading and cross-currents. He questions binary categories that seek to fix poetry too: roots/mobility, home/abroad, national/international, traditional/postmodernist. Hence the fact that Muldoon's Ireland fades into Muldoon's America and *vice versa*. "One Last Draw of the Pipe" seizes on a made-for-Muldoon passage in a Yeats letter: "Heard a piece of Roscommon folklore the other night. At some village or other, they lay pipes full of tobacco on the graves of the new buried in case they might like a draw of the pipe. A wild American indian kind of business it seems." And so the poem proves, as it conjures an Irish ghost "who may even now draw // a bead on me". "The Loaf" links Ireland and America from another ghostly angle:

> When I put my finger to the hole they've cut for a dimmer switch
> in a wall of plaster stiffened with horsehair
> it seems I've scratched a two-hundred-year-old itch
>
> *with a pink and a pink and a pinkie-pick.*
>
> When I put my ear to the hole I'm suddenly aware
> of spades and shovels turning up the gain
> all the way from Raritan to the Delaware
>
> *with a clink and a clink and a clinky-click* . . .

The Irish navvies who excavated the Delaware Canal, and often perished, appear to haunt Muldoon. In "The Loaf", parison and refrain gradually implicate the speaker's body in the painful history the poem evokes.

Yet, while Muldoon's Atlantic-hopping still questions origins, and perhaps national canons, this seems the most "Irish" of his recent collections. The gyre of imaginative return already discernible in *Hay* (1998) has become wider. *Moy Sand and Gravel* revisits primary autobiographical ground. Some lyrics (and the higher proportion of lyric to narrative is itself a gyre of return) even reconstitute his portraits of the artist as a child. The sestina "The Misfits", which links the film of that title with a jazz-loving, possibly boy-loving priest, against whom the speaker has been warned, is a *non serviam*. "The Turn", another sestina, conceives the artist's life as a digression beginning when the child-speaker "thought nothing of getting up and going out / while he was still halfway through a sentence". Here the film that signposts escape or revolt is *The Four Feathers*. So "return" is to a point of departure. As one of the sestina's rhyme-words, "turn" exemplifies the gyrations of Muldoon's poetics: "taking a turn // about the house", "sometimes not bothering to return / for an hour, two hours", "he'd taken it upon himself to turn / a stack of pear-boxes . . . into a bolster-humped camel", "every twist and turn / of the ergs and regs", "a scent powerful enough to turn / him around", "having him turn back inside to pick up his own sentence".

One context for Muldoon's latest twists and turns is that his dialectical poles have shifted. "America" is now more roots than frontier. Similarly, the Muldoon personae must at least confront, if not necessarily reconcile, *enfant terrible* or touring Tuareg with paterfamilias. Cyril Connolly's dictum about the pram in the hall also haunts *Moy Sand and Gravel*. An "old Biltrite pram" defiantly stars in the concluding long poem "At the Sign of

> Muldoon often quotes Yeats's reply when asked where he got his ideas from: "Looking for the next rhyme".

the Black Horse, September 1999". "The Ancestor", which broods and puns on "heirlooms", suggests that potentially calcifying forces – like authority, identity, tradition – stem from the impulse of the mind to familiarise rather than defamiliarise. Here the portrait of "no relation", a nineteenth-century Hungarian "great-grandmother", becomes so ominously familiar that she finally "lurches and looms / across the library".

There is also a gyre of return to accentuated verse-forms. Besides sestinas, *Moy Sand and Gravel* contains *terza rima*, the blend of *terza rima* and haiku pioneered in *Hay*, a range of stanzaic shapes and further variations on the sonnet. One variation, also evident in some stanzas, is a higher proportion of longer lines – up to more than twenty syllables. Variable line length has always been Muldoon's main concession to "free" verse, though invariably complicated by rhyme. Here the longer line is counterpointed by an intensification (if possible) of Muldoon's obsession with rhyme and refrain. These, as in the italicised refrain of "The Loaf", are ultimately the same thing: covered, like most rhetoric, by Louis MacNeice's term "repetition-devices". Muldoon's critics more often dwell on his preoccupation with language than on its semantic inseparability from his preoccupation with form. Perhaps he writes sestinas to make the point, as in the turns of "turn". The rhetorical figure revitalised by Muldoon's way with word, rhyme and refrain, a figure which may govern his poetry, is *antanaclasis*: i.e., repeating a word while shifting from one of its meanings to another. The plot of "The Misfits" is as likely to have been constructed from its rhyme-words as *vice versa*:

> "Blow all you like", my father turned on me. "Talk till you're blue
> in the face. I won't let you take a lift
> from the Monk. Blow all you like. I won't bend."
>
> The Monk had spent twenty-odd years as a priest in South Bend,
> his face priest-smooth except for a deep seam
> in his left cheek. Fred Grew said something strange about how he liked to
>   "lift
> his shirt-tail" . . .

Muldoon often quotes Yeats's reply when asked where he got his ideas from: "Looking for the next rhyme". Rhyme (like other formal parameters) is aleatory rather than restrictive: a fishing-net, a glimmer of the unknown. Repetition-devices belong to Heraclitus: you can't step into the same rhyme twice. The restriction of some free verse is that by eschewing repetition it may, paradoxically, stay in the same place. Who plays dice with blank pebbles? Muldoon's practice thus contrasts with Denise Riley's as expounded by Linda A. Kinnahan in the last issue of *Poetry Review* (not that he is any closer to so-called "new formalists"). Kinnahan praises Riley's work for offering "a total immersion into the palpable, visceral, material medium of words".

Yet the language Kinnahan applies to words is the language of the life to which they are bodily, cognitively, and culturally attached. Muldoon's poetry too can be described as "often about language itself and its forms, particularly its poetic forms". But he does not foreclose his epistemological scope in the belief that, because word and thing are not identical, there are no conduits between them. By inhabiting that unsettling between-place, Muldoon makes us think about language in all its senses. Nor does he assume that language controls us in ways that are wholly beyond poetry's control. To crack any system or code is again a matter of local specifics, local defamiliarisation ("*with a clink and a clink and a clinky-click*", "Fred Grew said something strange"). If, at one level, Muldoon's poetry constitutes a radical linguistic politics, it is because he continuously implies the norms from which his structures deviate or which they criticise. In contrast, merely to break syntax – not really a "chain" – or form – not really a prison – is a kind of blanket-bombing which underrates the resources of both.

Occasionally Muldoon's technical ingenuities, like his returns to "Moy", seem *déjà vu* if only by standards of self-reinvention which Muldoon himself has set. "Famous First Words", an alphabetical conceit, leaves me cold; as does the poem based on another parison: "As naught gives way to aught / and ox-hide gives way to chain-mail . . . " etc. Elsewhere, however, ingenuity "fetters" emotion as Donne said it should. "The Stoic", an elegy for a miscarried child, the book's middle poem, begins with "a burlapped fawn / half-way across the iced-over canal". This image surreally dissolves into "an Irish navvy" whose bandage has "a leak / of blood through the linen rag". The displacement and metamorphosis dramatise the difficulty of figuring "the afternoon last March/ when I got your call in St Louis". Partly by means of mirror-image rhymes, the poem then doubles back on itself to the original scene where refrain becomes poignantly oblique lament.

Muldoon's poetry implicitly aspires to fuse the linguistic precedent of Joyce with the formal precedent of Yeats. Yeats has already made guest-appearances in his work: now "At the Sign of the Black Horse" cheekily "rewrites" "A Prayer for My Daughter" in forty-five stanzas. Muldoon seems freshly interested in Yeats's manner of moving between public and private worlds, and of intertwining public events with family and ancestry. "A Grand Conversation" between "He" and "She" imitates and revises similar Yeatsian dialogues. It prepares for "At the Sign of the Black Horse" by constructing a bridge of possibility between *fearsad* and *verst*; i.e., between Muldoon's Irish past and that of his American-Jewish wife.

"At the Sign of the Black Horse" follows Yeats's rhyme-scheme but with longer and shorter lines, and enjambement between stanzas. The Muldoon-speaker replicates Yeats's role as unlikely baby-minder while an actual and political storm howls. He and his family picnic outside their house while observing the chaos of Canal Road flooded by Hurricane Floyd. The flood mutates into a fantasia of the flood of history, carrying ancestral voices, winners, losers, Holocaust-victims and other terrible débris. It also carries (in the manner of Yeatsian epilogue) refrains of the book's motifs and refrains. The poem's own refrains include Yeats's phrases: "My child sleeps on" and "The soul recovers radical innocence", both used to perhaps obvious ironic effect. Another refrain is the kind of bossy instruction we meet everywhere. Does the mix work?

> I looked up from our make-believe version of Boscobel Beach
> to a cauterised stump of sassafras or sycamore
>
> as the creel-carters piled more and more clay, hay, hair, spectacle-frames,
> *Willkommen*,

on to the line of carrioles and camions

by the edge of the flooded stream, those creel-carters imagining in excited
    reverie

the arches of the the bridge wrought with the motto *Arbeit Macht Frei*,

while I looked up through the swing

and swale of smoke, Please Leave A Message After The Beep ...

The Jewish material may be too much to internalise in the way that the "Prayer for My Daughter" template requires. And it seems glib to juxtapose everyday hectoring with the prescriptions of the concentration camp: this tonal blip being an indication that Muldoon's comedy and his seriousness are, for once, slightly at odds. His long poems depend on a number of balls being simultaneously but unnoticeably juggled. "The Mud Room" in *Hay* carries some of the same baggage more lightly. "At the Sign of the Black Horse" goes on rather too long, as do a number of its lines. Muldoon's true line has a lyric lilt and limit. Perhaps, too, "Cradle Song for Asher" already says it all in three couplets. Nonetheless, I confess, it took time before "The Mud Room" grew on me. Because Muldoon works so close to the grain of language and form, "making it new" while shedding none of poetry's inherited potential, every reading deepens the experience.

Product Displacement

JOHN TRANTER

John Ashbery, *Chinese Whispers*
Carcanet, £9.95, ISBN 1857546180

THE BRAND

John Ashbery is of course a person, an individual with distinctive characteristics. As he says in the poem "Too Much Sleep is Bad", "I don't have a chronic cough. / Cats don't drool over me". But there's also a product out there with the same brand-name, usually presented as just the surname, like "Ford", "Hoover", "macadam" or "silhouette".

"Ashbery" has been put together gradually over half a century in a largely unconscious collaborative project by a construction team of hundreds of magazine editors, publishers, reviewers, fellow-poets, and cultural and literary critics, as well as the person at the centre of it all. By now the brand-name "Ashbery" (a fortuitously unique misspelling) represents (as well as the person) both a career and its reification, a "body of work": some twenty-four books and countless interviews, articles, reviews and photographs.

"Ashbery" gradually emerged into the glare of public attention in the early 1970s, assisted by the publication of *An Anthology of New York Poets*. This collection, edited by the younger poets Ron Padgett and David Shapiro and published in June of 1970, mounted "Ashbery" at the prow of the "senior" "New York School" along with Edwin Denby, Kenneth Koch, James Schuyler and Frank O'Hara. The brand had earlier undergone various modifications. In the years of the McCarthy witch-hunts, of J. Edgar Hoover's secret frocks, of Eisenhower, it had spent a decade of redevelopment in France, where its early styling underwent an overhaul – originally a gentle, gawky kid producing sweet-natured and slightly wacky lyrics, it remodelled itself into a fierce intellectual with a vaguely European lineage, an un-American creature who would tear a living poem to shreds and reassemble the body parts into a cruel collage.

Eventually, after a sequence of stylistic shifts, the brand mutated into "The Readable Ashbery" during the northern fall of 1975, when the collection *Self-Portrait in a Convex Mirror* won the Big Three Prizes available to American poets: The Pulitzer, the National Book Critics Circle Award and the National Book Award.

John Ashbery (the person) has always maintained a discreet distance from the hoo-ha surrounding new product development, but he did admit – or at least Ashbery the interviewee admitted – that he doesn't think too much of the title poem in that book: in a 1985 interview with the present author he said "I've never really cared for 'Self-Portrait' very much, and I must say I didn't like it any more when I reread it. But I obviously had to put it in [to his 1985 *Selected Poems*] because people would expect it to be there".

THE CURRENT BRITISH MODEL

Carcanet's list is large and varied. There are, as with any list, earnest dullards aplenty, but also flashes of brilliance and rogue wit, often transatlantic: Kenneth Koch, Harry Mathews, Barbara Guest, and of course Ashbery. This book is the twenty-fourth release in the overall Ashbery poetry series (Carcanet has British retail rights for nineteen items) which, all-up, makes an average of one every two years since he began publishing nearly half a century ago.

The poems in *Chinese Whispers* are somewhat like the poems in his exacting early book *The Tennis Court Oath*, from Ashbery's "Paris years". Of the poems in that book he says "I did write them during a period when I didn't know what I wanted to do, when I began living in France and I was unused to the foreign environment and language and everything. They were really experiments which I didn't think would ever be published . . ." (*Jacket* magazine, No 2, January 1998). But the new poems are more readable, and by a wider audience, with the disparate fragments lashed together in a net of rambling discourse rather than left adrift as flotsam to broach and wreck the reader, as in the early book.

The tone of voice can easily accommodate a smart-guy wisecrack from the 1940s, and often swerves into Loony Tunes territory – Daffy Duck and Popeye both feature in earlier Ashbery poems. But the language can veer equally well from the scrappy to the scholarly. Here are a few of the plums that bedizen this lexical pudding: bedizened, slough, tetched, tisanes, trottoirs, ichor, hobson-jobson, codicil, columbarium, persiflating, inspissated, soffits, chancel, tesserae, wedgies, colibri, o'ersprent, voyante, clotured, and so on.

The dictionary is not likely to be much help. Does the title give us a pointer to the poet's concerns? Carcanet's blurb-writer seems to think so, but he or she is wrong. The parlour game called "Chinese Whispers" in England (and "English Whispers" in China?) is usually called "Telephone" in the US, which is perhaps why the oft-contrary author chose the more esoteric phrase, but even so these poems are not step-by-step narrative distortions of an originally simple story. The title in fact is borrowed from one of the poems in the book, and is as obstinately oblique as any of the other titles. "Little Sick Poem" is a robust piece of work, for example; "Portrait With a Goat" is entirely lacking in goats, though the doves which briefly appear remind one of the columbarium mentioned above, but then only etymologically. "From the Diary of a Mole" is a far cry from the usual mole-diary routine (we find three polar bears, a curlew's nest, a runt and some sleeping pagans, but no moles). And

"Ornery Fish" is an amiable and un-piscine excursus involving salad dressings, tea at twilight, and a wave "from which protrudes a tiny fist / clutching orange or yellow flowers". (Note: why so many animals?)

The title "Meet Me Tonight in Dreamland" is perhaps a clue. Most of these poems have a narrative, and the stories they tell are indeed like dreams:

> Someone brought in a tray of cakes which were distributed to the guests according to a fixed plan. "Here, this one's for you. Take it." I looked and saw only a small cat rolling in the snow of a darkened gutter. "If this is mine, then I don't want it." Abruptly the chords of a string quartet finished. I was on a shallow porch. The village movie palaces were letting out . . .
> ("Disagreeable Glimpses")

But why a "small" cat? Why is there snow in the gutter? Why is the gutter "darkened"?

On the other hand, would anyone think of asking Jackson Pollock why a particular splash of paint had been placed just so in a painting like *Blue Poles*, or *Lavender Mist*? It's the overall dynamic effect that seems to matter with Ashbery, as with Pollock, and the reader is encouraged to focus on large and tessellated networks of meaning, rather than on single phrases or linear sentences.

The Romantics (see below) introduced the idea of mood as the salient and crucial aspect of a painting. Perhaps it's a matter of mood with Ashbery, rather than individual brush-strokes. From near the concluding lines of some of the poems in this book:

> Not long ago I was in a quandary about this but now it's too late. The evening comes on and the aspens leaven its stars.
> ("A Nice Presentation")

> Our lives ebbing always towards the center,
> the unframed portrait.
> ("The Variorum Edition")

> Night, the sleeping animals –
> it all gets carted away,
> sooner or later . . .
> ("The Sleeping Animals")

> . . . it's all right, because it's all over.
> ("Disclaimer")

But the elegiac note only tells us what we already know, if we're paying attention to fleeting time. A T-shirt motto from the late twentieth century puts it succinctly: "Life's a bitch: first you grow old, then you die".

STYLING HISTORY

Here is John Ashbery reflecting on his role as artist in his poem "The Art of Speeding" (from *Hotel Lautréamont*, 1992): "I'm the cap and bells that don't belong. / A free-lance artist. The last and first of the romantics".

Romantics? The two most widely taken up inventions of the Industrial Revolution were steam engines and bottled scotch, but Romantic Poets come a close third. They were invented to soothe the bourgeoisie's anxiety at the sudden absence of God from the blasted landscapes they created in their pursuit of mass production and profit. Ashbery is an inheritor of the Romantic project; a kind of nonchalant and unobtrusively productive Wordsworth to O'Hara's nervous, intense and addicted Coleridge figure. His landscapes are large, sketchy structures – variegated, compacted, and full of a strange variety of animals, moody weather, and talking heads.

He may hint that they are "The Random Jottings of an Old Man", but this is another misleading title. The jottings are a topic in the poem, not its substance. Though some of his assemblages may seem random, their settings and backdrops frame a flow of natural and social energies (weather, passions, travel, music, cracker-barrel sayings, snippets of talk) all felted helter-skelter into a mass of overlapping insights.

Then the language that carries these insights is put through a compacter. This tightening-up of the link between layers of identification is a version of the process whereby a simile is compressed into a metaphor, from "is like" to "is": "the waves on the surface of the sea far below a high vantage point look like wrinkles on an old person's skin, and their rushing movement seen from such a distance is like a mere crawling motion" becomes in the compression-chamber of Tennyson's magisterial technique "the wrinkled sea beneath him crawls".

So a lesser poet might have written "The foam at the edges of the waves lapping on the shore looked like embroidery". With Ashbery there's an extra metaphorical twist, borrowed from the mid-twentieth-century French surrealists: "The embroidered hems of waves annoyed the shoreline . . ." ("Disagreeable Glimpses")

The surprising mundanity of the surreal world is perhaps its most uncanny aspect. Yes, and Ashbery takes that mundanity further, too, until it's really weird.

MODEL DEFECT WARNING

Some patients cannot tolerate even small doses of this medication. There is a problem: the problem of meaning. For a hundred thousand years, words have been used to communicate meanings and messages. We might as well admit that the two-page prose poem "Truth Gleams" is incomprehensible, as well as being entirely in quotation marks (so perhaps someone else wrote or spoke it): "'Nor will I know what to eat, when she rounds the curve of bananas. The altar offered little but idle chitchat. How far you've come if it's autumn, and the plagues will surround you nervously, waiting for an opening. It could be anything, or just about anything, it seems . . .'"

So it seems.

Other readers have suggested that Ashbery's poems sometimes comment on themselves as they unfold – and indeed this piece could be doing just that, admitting that it "could be . . . just about anything, it seems".

I don't know what to say about that. Perhaps Archibald MacLeish was right way back in 1926, in his "Ars Poetica": "A poem should not mean / But be". John Ashbery was born the following year; and the product cycle began.

Sorely Missed

STUART KELLY

**Somhairle Macgill-Eian / Sorley Maclean, *Dáin do Eimhir / Poems to Eimhir*
Edited by Christopher Whyte**
Association of Scottish Literary Studies, £12.50, ISBN 0948877502

SORLEY MACLEAN (SOMHAIRLE MACGILL-EIAN) is widely acknowledged as the pre-eminent Scottish Gaelic poet of the twentieth century, not just for the palpable beauty of his lyric writing, but for the manner in which he resituated Gaelic poetics within a wider, European, and Modernistic context, without sacrificing its indigenous traditions and methods. This commitment can be seen in poem XX of Christopher Whyte's important scholarly edition of *Dáin do Eimhir* (*Poems to Eimhir*) which closes looking for

> dáintean sam faicte chrois
> bh' air Yeats is Blok is Uilleam Ros.

> [poems where one would see the cross
> borne by Yeats and Blok and William Ross][1]

These figures are present not only as technical "elder brothers in the Muse", but serve as symbols of an archetypal myth; the poet whose work is the direct product of the depredations and torments of unrequited love. For Iain Crichton Smith, who translated the poetry, MacLean was firmly in the tradition of the lyric love poet, a Gaelic Catullus.

MacLean was born on Raasay in 1911, and studied under Herbert Grierson at Edinburgh University. Although he was later to play down the influence of Grierson's vigorous promotion of the Metaphysical poets, there are undeniable traces of the cerebral yet confessional stance ("an eanchainn shingilte's an cridhe sgàinte", "the single brain and the split heart"), as well as dazzling volte-faces of imagery that recall Donne's conceits. In 1934 he met Hugh MacDiarmid (Christopher Grieve), the dynamo of the Scottish Renaissance, whose work he already knew and who became a more persistent and openly acknowledged influence: indeed, he described the lyrics of *Sangshaw* (1925) and *Penny Wheep* (1926) as "supreme ... completely new and unbelievable ... a miracle and mystery". The men shared a similar political outlook, although it would be more appropriate to describe MacLean as anti-Fascist rather than a committed Communist. By 1944, when Russia put down the Polish rebellion, MacLean became "politically as well as aesthetically disgusted" with his long lyric epyllion "An Cuilithionn" (The Cuillin), which radiated out from Skye to survey the rise of Fascism in Europe and located its possible redemption thus:

> Có bheir faochadh dhan àmhghar
> mur tig an t-Arm Dearg sa chàs seo?
> [Who will give respite to the agony
> unless the Red Army comes in this extremity?][2]

---

1. Editor's translation
2. MacLean's translation

Wounded three times in active service in North Africa, he returned to Scotland to teach, first at Boroughmuir, then Plockton. His later work was intermittent – the silence was attributed by him to "my addiction to an impossible lyric ideal". However, after his retirement in 1972 his importance was gradually appreciated, with the Saltire Scottish Book of the Year award in 1991 for his Collected Poems, *O Choille gu Bearradh* (*From Wood to Ridge*), which was also a Poetry Book Society Special Recommendation. MacLean died in 1996.

Forty-nine of the sixty-one *Poems to Eimhir* appeared in the 1943 *Dàin do Eimhir agus Dàin eile* (*Poems to Eimhir and Other Poems*), and, by the time of the *Collected Poems*, the sequence is scattered throughout the volume. The original 1943 collection was a less than perfect edition, and even included a note on the "vicissitudes of publication" – MacLean was wounded, and the publisher Douglas Young imprisoned at the time. Whyte's edition restores all but one (lost) poem, with full bibliographical reference to the variant readings and copy-text, as well as detailed notes on the composition, allusions, and history behind the sequence. One minor quibble would be the decision not to reprint the illustrations by William Crosbie which appeared in the 1943 volume: images so bizarre that Ronald Black remembers dropping the book through shock. But this is a minor, minor quibble in comparison to the immense service Whyte has performed in restoring both the text and its centrality to twentieth-century poetry.

Dàin do Eimhir is a sustained and exquisitely lyrical meditation on love, poetry, and politics. It is mordant, celebratory, elegiac, and intense; and debates in itself the nature of commitment, the Platonic relationship between physical and spiritual beauty, and the lessons learnt in pain. It moves from the local (the imagined shores of poem XLII) and the universal (poem XLV ranging as far as Betelgeuse). Poem XXX, in which, for the beloved, MacLean imagines a revolutionary Scotland cleansed of the "sgreamhalachd luchd na maoin" (loathsomeness of capitalists), enacts an astonishing and hyperbolic switch, unlike anything contemporaneous:

> dh'èighinn 'nad bhànrainn Albann thu
> neo-ar-thaing na Poblachd ùir.
>
> [I would proclaim you queen of Scotland
> in spite of the new Republic.][3]

It must be admitted that the English reader, approaching even MacLean's own translations, may find the work slightly thin. MacLean made no attempt whatsoever to replicate in English the rhyme schemes, textures of register or chains of phonetic effect which characterise the Gaelic. The crystalline compactness of MacLean's lyrics probably cannot be recaptured. To give just a flavour of this, it is worth looking at poem XLIV:

> ruiginn an sin crè-ghaol
> mo chèille luiadhe
>
> [there I would reach the love-core
> of my ardent devotion][4]

---

3. MacLean's translation
4. Editor's translation

Here, as Whyte points out, "gaol", "ciall", and "luaidh" can all mean "love", and a theoretically possible translation would be "I would reach the [literally] clay-love / of my love of love"; while "ciall" may also mean "reason" (thus adding another layer of Platonic connotation). Poetry which can deploy all the semantic nuance, all the splitting and coalescing of language, is doing exactly what poetry should: and as such it is forever locked into its own language.

By contrast, MacLean introduced much of the wider poetic world into Gaelic literature, and it would be fitting and encouraging if this new edition introduced MacLean to the wider world. Likewise, it would be a positive step if this edition paved the way for a complete text of MacLean's *oeuvre*, edited with similar sensitivity and precision. MacLean offers a poetry which is intelligent without being arch, and where commitment never teeters into sloganising. Above all, he captures the great paradox of love poetry, the point at which the limits of expression are confronted and evaded: "Chaidh mo ghaol ort tha bàrdachd [My love for you has gone beyond poetry]".

New Djinns for Old

JANE GRIFFITHS

Alison Croggon, *Attempts at Being*
Salt £9.95, ISBN 1876857420
Kate Fagan, *The Long Moment*
Salt £8.95, ISBN 1876857390
Jill Jones, *Screens Jets Heaven*
Salt £9.95, ISBN 1876857226
Kate Lilley, *Versary*
Salt £8.95, ISBN 1876857153
Sophie Levy / Leo Mellor, *Marsh Fear / Fen Tiger*
Salt £8.95, ISBN 1876857072

TWO OF THE six poets in these recent collections from Salt Publishing are bold enough to include within their work a direct reflection on the lyric. In Alison Croggon's *Attempts at Being*, this takes the form of an extended meditation, "On Lyric", a series of aphoristic observations teasingly sandwiched between a one-line opening section, "The poet asserts", and a still shorter closing section, consisting of a single word: "Nevertheless". In the intervening sections, she offers various definitions and denials: lyric "is not a category but a dimension of a poem / lyric might be thought of as the field of force of a poem", "lyric is the desire towards the invisibility of the self", "the poetry of touch", "a metaphor for feeling"; it is "indefensible", it is "not reality / it is real". However, the definitions themselves are less important than the way in which the opening line qualifies them, so that the assertion of certainties itself becomes an experiment in phrasing. "On Lyric" doesn't so much define Croggon's position as illustrate her characteristic assumption of a persona. In her work for radio and her stage-play "The Breach", a plethora of voices interrupt and modify one another, not through interaction but rather by juxtaposition. Like each of these intertwined narratives, her lyrics may be read as "a way of putting it", or justly "attempts at being".

In Kate Fagan's *The Long Moment* the reference to lyric is altogether more fleeting.

Where "a river repeats, / one narrative of urbanite getaway", "lyric interjects / demanding specific / impatient approval // quick like junk, memorial about position / and meaning". This untitled lyric itself, one of the long sequence "return to a new physics", is an almost outrageously apt description of Fagan's manner of seeing. The poems in the first section of the book, "Calendar", record what seems initially a near-overwhelming assault and battery of impressions, consisting of objects and perception of those objects in equal measure: "Cars glint almost charmingly along the river. Buildings have their / impressive disregard for sound. Everything happens because of / this chance encounter, a series of circles a street sign a long / pavement or music wrapping into branches, apertures of air." As in her aperçu of the lyric, such "junk" or cumulative observation becomes both subject and means of thought; her work fuses "the mattered thing" which is made memorial and the process of memorializing. The danger of such insistent reformulation is that it becomes self-reflexive as the Red King's dream, but Fagan avoids this by her fierce inclusivity; the stunning "Ecologue" mediates a beached whale into a reflection on the making of history, granting the catastrophe and the perception of it equal weight, and clearly demonstrating, as she says elsewhere, that "nothing stands for nothing". Fagan's poetry creates an exciting synaesthesia between thought and feeling. It has what she calls "the sound of a great *improvisation*"; it is wholly original.

By contrast, Jill Jones' earlier work in *Screens Jets Heaven* can seem insufficiently improvised. In "Hyperventilating in the Supermarket", for example, she sets up with neat descriptive irony the expected opposition between the shiny displays of Christmas shopping and the "others" who "are dying in queues". Even where her overtly moral impulse is abandoned for a more meditative tone, a poem's end often seems implicit in its beginning. Her later work, however, is increasingly open to irresolution. Sometimes this is itself made too explicit, as when, at the conclusion of "A white beach", the poem's holiday mood is encapsulated in a kite which "bobs in clear air above the shallows, / because no-one cares how far it went / when you tossed it against the wind". At other times, however, Jones allows her delightfully precise and evocative descriptions of cityscape and landscape to stand uninterpreted, and this makes her work a pleasure to read.

While Jones can sometimes seem to be too sure of her conclusions, for Kate Lilley the conclusion is always what has been left unsaid. This is most apparent in "Mint in Box: A Pantoum Set", the sequence at the centre of *Versary*. With its off-beat repetitions, the pantoum is the perfect form to emphasise Lilley's habitual use of the line as a unit of meaning whose meaning is oblique, as in the opening stanzas of the third pantoum: "There's a knack to fixing the drapes / spring cleaning doesn't answer // unless you include prior convictions / reward me with infatuation // spring cleaning doesn't answer / sensitivity can't help suffering // reward me with infatuation / should that be complaint or compliant". When the changes are rung so insistently, attention necessarily shifts from what is written to the manner of writing. Yet if "versary" on one level refers to the recycling of poetic forms, or perhaps to the creation of a store-house of such forms, the poetic equivalent of a bestiary, it also suggests the topsy-turvy overturning of expectations. In Lilley's work all these things are the case. The epigraph to "Lady in the Dark", from Thomas Wilson's *Arte of Rhetorique* (1560), suggests that the "store-house" sense of "versary" is foremost. Wilson writes that "The places of memorie are resembled unto Waxe and Paper . . . The utterance and using of them, is like unto reading". He refers to a memorizing technique common in the Renaissance, in which the object or the fact or the line of verse to be remembered is mentally "placed" somewhere in a familiar physical location – say, on the chest of drawers in the spare bedroom – from which it can easily be retrieved. This offers a clue to reading the seemingly oblique but charged poems of "Lady in the Dark". The poems describe the memory places, rather than the emotion associated with them, which is left for the reader to infer. The allusions to cinematic genres and individual films function as the decontextualized lines of the pantoum set do, as indicators of what lies beneath. In thoroughly Renaissance style, Lilley insists that the best reading is between the lines. *Versary* is a mistress-piece of disguise, a fine mint of phrases, a teasing presentation of new wine in old bottles, or new djinns for old.

Where Lilley is concerned to test poetic forms and reading-methods, Sophie Levy is concerned primarily with words pure and simple – or perhaps that should be "rarely simple and never pure". In *Marsh Fear/Fen Tiger* her fierce awareness that language lacks innocence is sometimes overwhelming, as in "Hunting the Winter", whose first stanza, set in a library, includes "*Seasons of mists*. Well, yes. / Inside a cloud as much as out. Stale breath. No *fruitfulness*", and which goes on to appropriate Wilde, mnemonic, and fairy tale: "The howls begin. Books fall open. The unspoken in pursuit / of the unspeakable. *Calloo callay hurrah* and *tally-ho*. Nothing really. / The quick fox jumps sentence, Red Riding Hood to Snow White, runs into // winter". For all that, Levy's sharp linguistic sense has a real forcefulness at times, as in the fine "Epithalamium", or the third part of "Stammer", where her variations on familiar phrases serve as an acknowledgedly provisional means of making sense of a difficult world. When she allows her own voice to be heard, it is well worth hearing.

Levy's companion poet in the same volume, Leo Mellor, is noticeably quieter. He has an admirably precise eye and ear for the telling detail, as in the title-poem, which begins with the apparently impossibly romantic "My love and I went riding", but ends in a different register: "On return, an arrowhead / of crows lifting from up the road, / and a line of hairs stiff as reeds / welded cold on a neck". His startling accuracy belies his conclusion in "Slate", where he writes of words as "nothing beyond the splay / of voltage lost, / settling into sedimentary air". His own voltage is considerable, so that his recognition of the fragility of communication here prompts a response along Croggon's lines: "Nevertheless".

Did You Pack this Bag Yourself?

JOHN REDMOND

W. N. Herbert, *The Big Bumper Book of Troy*
Bloodaxe, £8.95, ISBN 1852246030

THE STRANGE TITLE announces not an anthology of especially boisterous Iliad-translations, but W. N. Herbert's fourth full collection from Bloodaxe. In one respect the title fits: the book is indeed "big": 160 pages of poems, some in Scots, most in English. While references to "Troy" pointedly occur, anyone after a sustained meditation on Homer will be disappointed. The volume is more in the nature of a travelogue recording Herbert's experiences outside Britain (principally Moscow, St. Petersburg, Madrid, Donegal and Crete) and inside (principally Dundee and his new lighthouse home on the Tyne).

The book is divided into five parts, the last of which, "Troytoon", is devoted to Dundee, his home "toon" (Herbert's own usage). Signalling the book's apparent theme, "The Death of Pieface", from this last section, is prefaced by a famous passage from Patrick Kavanagh's

"Epic". There the Irish poet, doubtful of the value of parochial squabbles, hears Homer's ghost whisper: ". . . I made the *Iliad* from such / A local row". Herbert's poem, duly encouraged, begins: "Dundee is Troy – ut's true, ask ony / MacSchliemann o thi Tay". The concluding sentence of Kavanagh's poem, not quoted by Herbert, is "Gods make their own importance". For Kavanagh the brisk point of equating village and *Iliad* is to assert the arrogant power of poetic creation. For Herbert the point is altogether vaguer – throughout the book he compares many places, not just Dundee, to Troy. The practical purpose served, however, is to unify – faintly – otherwise unrelated experiences in various parts of the world.

Apart from the MacDiarmid-inspired experiments in Scots, Herbert's macaronic diction, jumpy sense of the line, hectic cosmopolitanism and devotion to public space, strongly echo Tony Harrison circa *The Loiners*. To such elements is added a dose of cartoon fantasy, as in "The Entry of Don Quixote into Newcastle upon Tyne":

> . . . He charges the Magpies during
> a crucial fixture, convinced that eleven
> cannot be a lucky number. Quixote is played,
> as always by Miguel de Unamuno.
> The Toon Army chant "Get back, get back,
> get back to Le Pays Basque!"

Herbert's humor is rarely understated; more Ben Elton than Jack Dee, as unrelenting, in its way, as the "Ho Ho Ho" of a High Street Santa Claus. It is also over-inclusive. In a poem dealing with Mayakovsky, for instance, he offers the phrase "I Herbert Read you", while English football supporters are dismissed as the "Smarmy Army". The awkward fun extends to neologisms like "touristicals", "drinkupmanship", "Hogmillennium", "mausolinoleum", "lookielikie", "ranchalows", "Instantinople" and "Dan Darevitch".

The main ethic of the book is accumulation – especially of exotic words (like the above, plus foreign phrases, place-names, artist-names). Because the I-narrator is relatively passive, rarely engaged in a specific task, being led by friends or tourguides, the main emotional vibrations of the poems are often the movement from one exotic word to another. The opening of "Foreign Literature" is fairly typical:

> Past the Smirnoff house and over the river,
> past the church where Akhmatova worshipped,
> we drove down the Street of the Golden Horde
> that leads to the office of *Foreign Literature*.
> I faced a portrait of Yuri Gagarin
> Picasso had sketched in the guts of a pigeon.

At times, an image will genuinely emerge from this magpie inclusiveness, as in "Crossing the Youza" where ". . . the little shrubs / grow out of the church's brick-bare belfry / like hair out of an old man's ears". Occasionally, the poems will offer a detail of documentary interest: "They used to develop the giant photographs, / Marxian super-icons, in the public baths . . ." More often, though, the effect of such exotica, at once specific and barely con-textualized, is curiously numbing, like being shown hundreds of holiday photographs at once.

While the poems are often organized on the level of form, they are seldom organized on the level of analysis. Those that succeed are either short like "Ormos Almirou" and "Sciffy", or else refrain from moral-drawing and overt commentary like "Spooner Vale" (a clever play with spoonerisms) and "At MacDiarmid's Tomb" (an exercise in found material). When his poems reach, as the opening of "Walking Home at Midnight" does, for a penetrating statement, the effect can be clumsy:

> There are places you will never be at home
> and times when you should know it
> or go wrong somewhere
> under where you think.

Lines three and four (what do they mean?) illustrate his difficulty with using, in Seamus Heaney's phrase, "a line like bare wire", and may help to explain his distracting use of adornment elsewhere. At the beginning the book carries a quotation from the Russian composer Alfred Schnittke, which speaks of the value of a "unified style", what the blurb calls "a disrespectful polstylist unity". One would like to believe in syntheses of this sort, but Jarrell's ghost comes whispering (I paraphrase): "an artist is eventually tempted to create a form into which everything – all facets of his personality and experience, earnest, trivial, noble, sly, learned, comic, high and low – will fit. And he succeeds. He creates it – and he discovers it is not an art form".

Let it be Small Enough

SARA LUNDQUIST

Jorie Graham, *Never*
Ecco (HarperCollins), $22.95, ISBN 0060084715
Barbara Guest, *Miniatures and Other Poems*
Wesleyan University Press, $12.95, ISBN 0819565962

THE POEMS IN Pulitzer Prize winner Jorie Graham's ninth collection, *Never*, record elemental outdoor encounters with the here and now, always changing in the instant of perception, always evading language and thought, always sifting into the wind. The poems, nonetheless, fiercely desire to witness the world's restless, reckless, abandonment of the here and now: surging forward on dozens of progressive verbs, verbal nouns, verbal adjectives, racing to stay current. Her lines are long; the prefix "re-" pushed to an enjambed line's-end, re-enforcing the point of lineation: dramatic returns from a point reached. Graham's wild world and turbulent mind are "re-/sistant", "re-/entering", "re-/peated", "re-/presenting", "re-/infolding", "re-/gardless", "re-/turning". Following American poets before her – Whitman, Stevens, and Moore – she turns ocean-ward: to sun, waves, gulls, kelp-beds, tide pools, wind, mist, spray, shifting and sucking sands, seeking a solitary colloquy with nature. Like the Impressionist painters, she worked *en plein-air*, training the pen to depend on the eye: looking, looking, then writing, then looking again and writing again, and reminding herself to listen also, and again: "[put / birdchatter in]". This "impression-ist" combination of concentration and fidelity to change evidences the poet's need to marry objectivity and subjectivity. "I try," she writes, "in my acts of composition, to experience subjectivity and objectivity at their most frayed and fruitful and morally freighted juncture . . . I believe accurate representation of this juncture is possible, and that character is involved in approaching that border". This is electrifying, uncomfortable, daily work, undertaken on behalf of the human species, in fear for the fate of the earth:

> I am a frequency, current flies through. One has
> to ride
> the spine.
> No peace [of mind] [of heart], among the other
> frequencies. How often and how hard are the answerings.
> (from "Ebbtide")

> light floods a bit, one feels a center, all directions shine from it,
> [is a center sought?] I mean, because I'm one of the few,
> you know, right here for you,
> going on like this, in America,
> where the dream is of course gone because it has
> too much power, one of the few,
> hiding from disbelief,
> and it's not a dark place, you know, though so inward,
> and it takes up all the room.
> (from "By the Way")

Irony is noticeably lacking in this volume, as if Graham felt that the essential disbelief lurking in irony were no longer affordable, albeit so pervasive that one must "hide" from it. Belief is the crux: Graham's epigraph quotes Keats upon seeing the Lake District for the first time: "How can I believe in that? Surely it cannot be?" Beauty, wildness, and the know-ableness of nature are just what the poems struggle to believe in. Indeed, in the year 2002, Graham feels a special urgency in her investigations into ancient issues of perception and representation. "During the 1850s," she notes "while Darwin was concluding *On the Origin of Species*, the rate of extinction [for species] is believed to have been one every five years. Today, [it] is estimated at one every nine minutes . . . I was haunted by . . . that nine-minute span – which might amount to the time it takes to read any poem here before you . . . [The book] is written up against the sensation of what is now called 'ecocide'." Any particular "here and now" will never return to the perceiving subject, but even poets who lament this strict fact have trusted that similar moments in similar vitally-alive natural settings will be accessible to human beings, now and always. Yet *Never*'s celebrations feel elegiac, final, and heartsick, as if Graham were watching the word "never" move into its fullest, flattest, most intransigent meaning:

> I cannot of course come back. Not to this. Never.
> It is a ghost posed on my lips. Here: never.
> (from "Prayer")

Poems of particular note are "Prayer," "Kyoto," and two from the final section, "High Tide," and "The Taken-Down God", which ends on a rapturous litany of "you" and "now". Like Whitman, Graham seduces the reader to a complex sense of nowness: the now of experience, the now of the pen scratching, the now of reading. "I am with you, and know how it is," says Whitman. "[T]his voice which is called 'I' will say to you: now: / now: [can you do *that?*]: now: [do you feel it][there in // your face, in your palms]: *now*", says Graham. Again, nearly 150 years of stress (to the environment and to communication) inhere in the difference between Whitman's calm, companionable statement and Graham's fevered momentum, agitated by italics, escalated by colon after colon, slowed by aggrieved and tender asides bracketed in.

What vertigo a reader feels in turning from Graham to Barbara Guest, two poets quite divergent in their routes of difficulty. Guest, since the publication of her lavish *Selected Poems* (1995, Sun & Moon) has opened the rich coffers of her imagination to write no less than seven books, each small, concentrated, radiant. *Miniatures and Other Poems*, is the latest in this extraordinary late-life surge of creativity and poetic license. Each miniature poem collected here reveals an intimate portion of its author's intense and intensely literary memory. Like Chekhov, quoted as an epigraph, Guest is "an ardent defender of miniature pieces". The word "piece" expresses two meanings: a single composition in paint, poetry, or prose, and, alternately, a detached part of something larger. Just so, these poems are complete in themselves, and suggestive of large realms: whole eras of time passed, erstwhile linguistic flowerings, the work of other authors, long-gone fashions of dress and sensibility, styles of painting, music and architecture, mythology, junkets and revolutions, manners and mores.

While Graham confronts ocean and wind, turning resolutely toward nature and experience, Guest turns inward, indoors and deep into artifice, making again of the already made, distilling, compressing. Graham wants here and now; Guest many many theres and thens, relishing curious conventions and constructions in phrases like "Swete be sound and soothing", and "be wrestled and / fielded on gold champs" and "His eyes shine red in his kingdom".

The miniature must be most ardently defended *because* it is little, because it might turn precious, sentimental, dainty, cute, nostalgic, derivative. That Guest avoids *all* of these pitfalls attests to her humor and compassion, her trust, not in allusion, but in allusiveness. One responds to a poem like "Blue Arthur" by deeply sharing its cultural provenance, and by recognizing with sympathy that even the great King can be struck by ordinary lovesickness, and must pay his dues:

> Aroused from bed with movement around him.
> Fasted and lay with malade. Waited with poem
> folded into sorrow.
> Hollow, blue morning.
>
> Cloth overhangs daytime
>
> Kingdom of Blue Arthur.
>
> Dismayed lightness.
>
> Woman walks solitary arrayed in grey velveteen, door open for her.

Although I know of no actual painting that the poem might reference, it feels ekphrastic: a "miniature 'blue-period' portrait of Arthur (clutching poem) with unnamed mysterious woman". A bit of a joke, a keepsake, a fragment shored. So does Guest choose, from the immensity of cultural memory, moments to tease into wakefulness, focused by the smallest frame art can supply. Each of her miniatures occupies its page wryly, irresistibly, elegantly declining ego and grandiosity. Chaucer, Chekhov, Virgil, Ovid, Keats, Coleridge, medieval monks, the Provençal poets, Aalto, the art of photography, Finnish opera, Finnish architecture, the French Revolution, the Industrial Revolution, Colonial America, Schöenberg, Liszt, and Wagner – all are brought to Guest's test of miniaturization, her microcosmic sensibility. "And there is where the risk lies," she writes, "in that balancing act, so filled with fervor and terror as the little word is placed on its spool of light".

Could it be that "Autobiography" is a miniature *self*-portrait of Guest in the 21st century? If so, Guest's readers have reason to celebrate her groundedness, her still-vital perception, her at-last-rewarded implacability, the enviable triumph that by now, "most of the work [is] elective". She lives, perhaps literally there in California, in a "warm / house" beside which "a cocoanut tree grows". And, she claims simply: "[u]nderfoot is secure, / part of the made-up plan". For her, there is a "[b]ar of ivory light suspended". In her eighties, Guest catches for language what inheres of a lifetime of loved art, gleaning from her heart and brain their personal, dream-like, art-infused contents. Ezra Pound, concerned in old age with what can be kept and what must be surrendered, wrote: "What thou lovest well remains, / the rest is dross / What thou lov'st well shall not be reft from thee / What thou lov'st well is thy true heritage". A disinterested, yet amused and passionate love pervades these little poems: Guest's is a very ripe, very piquant late harvest, both rich and spare, no room for dross.

Jobs and Services

PATRICK MCGUINNESS

Andrew Motion, *Public Property*
Faber, £12.99, ISBN 0571215343

ANDREW MOTION'S SKILL lies in unfolding and accumulating ideas, in poems that build up with careful modulations of thought and feeling, intimate but rarely mawkish. He is good also at putting language to those compound feelings that never stay long enough to be named, or look like small doses of something definite, as when regret swerves into grief, or an imprecisely melancholic thought finds itself grounded in something too painful to face head-on. His best work has a way of looking that changes what is looked at without betraying or distorting it; and I would say that there are moods and sensations in a Motion poem that one perhaps doesn't find in words in anybody else's. These show up as well as ever in this new collection, *Public Property*. The short poem "Diving" creates a sense of having all the time in the world to express itself, and feels slow and distended while being tightly written and sharply observed:

> […]
> Faint but definite
> heat of the universe

flutters my skin,
quick fish apply
as something to love
what with their heads
of unworldly gold,
plankton I push

as easy way through
would be dust or dew
in the world behind
if that mattered at all,
which is no longer true,
with its faces and cries.

"The Fox Provides for Himself" shows Motion's ability to dissect emotions, thoughts, movements in ways that are at once precise and unfamiliar. The poem tracks the movement of a fox – "a shadow worked itself loose at the edge of our world. / Not a shadow. A fox…" – across a field of vision, tracking also the thoughts and feelings that accompany it:

back to the neighbour's wall, and as he leaped he seemed
to hang on the bricks – slackened, to show his skeleton must
have somehow slipped from his body, or so I thought,
watching the breeze re-open his fur, and waiting to see how
he dropped – hardly a fox now, more like a trickle of rust –
my hand still holding your hand as he went, then letting go.

The dominant mode of this book is elegiac – poems for Diana, The Queen Mother, W. G. Sebald, and, among the best in the book, for his parents-in-law – but *Public Property* lacks the sustained depth and ambition of *Salt Water* (his last collection) or the rawness of his early books. This is partly because of the official poems, which seem uncertain of their relation to the private world, where real poetry (or at any rate Motion's own best work) begins but soon moves out of. With the laureate poems, it's the inverse: an attempt to make the public dimension intimate, to follow the ritualistic surface of royalty as if it had a vanishing-point in some deep inner life worth celebrating. Except it doesn't; rather it vanishes into layer upon layer of surface. Where a laureate like Ted Hughes (dedicatee of a poem in this book), priapic and full of primal fire, would have believed in blood and soil, divine rights *et al.*, in these cagey times Motion believes more in the *need* to believe in it. Motion's laureate poems distance themselves from their subjects:

THE PALACE BOMBED: then comes the blast
and choking life that lands you where
you *look East Enders in the face* – […]
and you *like one of us* – or like enough
to make a crowd of wind-frayed kids
and peering mums, the husbands jostling

with the press-men in their burly coats,
all think you are. And thank their lucky stars.

Here the focus is on the facticity of the magic, and many of the laureate poems contain mention of cameras, film, flashbulbs, newspapers, as if to emphasise the showy superficiality of the whole charade. What Motion gestures to is the image of the image, the perception of the perception: everything is attenuated, filtered, seen through as soon as seen. In this sense at least these poems may be more subversive than they at first let on. Even their disposition in the volume suggests irony, with the personal poems enfolding the public like inverted commas, separating them off in a kind of poetic quarantine. In a sense, the royal poems hitch a ride on the emotional depth of poems like "In Memory of Mervyn Dalley", and several, such as the poem for the marriage of the Wessexes, have been left out altogether – perhaps judging that there are occasions when the subject conspicuously fails to live up to the poem.

There are also verses that look like tesselations of *Daily Mail* soundbites. This one – from "Remember This" – casts the Queen Mother as a normal granny transubstantiated by selfless duty (rather than, for instance, an unreconstructed grasper after privilege and tight as a gnat's chuff to boot):

> the century's eyes
> of homage and duty
> which understand best
> the persistence of love.

Motion has extended the range of laureate subjects by writing poems for the TUC, Children in Need and the Salvation Army, and has promoted poetry's profile across Britain in ways that mark a departure from the traditional role of royal in-house poet. But the problem with the institution appears in the contrast between his poem for the TUC Congress (tellingly titled "In a Perfect World") and the poems for the Queen Mother. There's something inanely reactionary (and very New Labour) about seeing concern for working conditions as idealistic and utopian, while pretending that the Queen Mother was normal and down to earth. By far the best of the laureate poems (and fine by any standards) is the poem to Diana, "Mythology", where the mythological and the soap operatic dimensions (hounds and newshounds) merge without bathos or distortion:

> And you? Your life was not your own to keep
> or lose. Beside the river, swerving underground,
> the future tracked you, snapping at your heels;
> Diana, breathless, hunted by your own quick hounds.

Motion has done more for the institution of poet laureate than it has done for him, and he has stooped to the challenge with grace and skill. It's a dirty job but someone's got to do it, as they say about the Queen. Or have they?

Mandelstam's Gardener

MICHAEL CAINES

David Morley, *Scientific Papers*
Carcanet, £7.95, ISBN 1857545672
David Morley and Andy Brown, eds, *Of Science*
Worple Press, £16.00, ISBN 095309474X

IN THE TRADITIONAL enmity between art and science, art has unfairly stood for any aspect of human behaviour that would seem out of place in the stereotypical physics lab. The anthropologist Claude Levi-Strauss rightly argues that a separation occurred between science and "mythological thought" in the seventeenth and eighteenth centuries that was essential to the progress of the former. Nevertheless, he observes, "natural and cultural phenomena" such as poetry, "may share formal characteristics, without reducing either science or art to merely a flat reflection of the other".

Charles Dodgson's 1879 mathematical paper, "Euclid and His Modern Rivals", caught Robertson Davies's eye, as "a serious and excellent contribution to Euclidean geometry"; but the mathematical world was offended by it because it contained a number of jokes, and the mathematical world does not admit the existence of jokes. To Davies, "This seems to be a case in which Dodgson and [his literary alter ago, Lewis] Carroll became dangerously mingled". Usually, Dodgson's technical treatises on maths were received "with respect, if not rapture, by the people who could understand them". In Philip Pullman's *The Subtle Knife*, the dichotomy is worse still, with morality taking the side of Dodgson/Carroll's sense of humour against mathematics and empirical investigation. "Everything about this is embarrassing" says a scientist (and former nun). "D'you know how embarrassing it is to mention good and evil in a scientific laboratory? Have you any idea? One of the reasons I became a scientist was not to have to think about that kind of thing". It is as if Wordsworth and Coleridge never wrote in their Preface to the 1802 *Lyrical Ballads* that "poetry is the breath and finer spirit of all knowledge; it is the impassioned expression which is in countenance of all science".

David Morley and Andy Brown, editors of a slim volume of poems called *Of Science*, take the 1802 *Lyrical Ballads* as the model for their "unmisted" poetic engagement with scientific phenomena, quoting these lines:

> If the labours of Men of Science should ever create any material revolution, direct or indirect, in our condition, and in the impressions we habitually receive, the Poet will sleep then no more than at present, but . . . follow the steps of the Man of Science . . .

In this view, the act of "carrying sensation into the midst of the objects of Science itself" is poetry's mission. Poetry, in this assessment, must humbly take its place as the vessel of witness, not "material revolution"; and this is generally how the relationship between art and science has stood ever since – hence the resentful teasing. It is both a "useful" role and a scientifically sound one: accurate, meaningful observation. As Osip Mandelstam puts it in the epigraph to David Morley's first full-length collection of poems, *Scientific Papers*, "Here the demands of science correspond to one of the most fundamental aesthetic laws". But the "birdcall" of *Of Science* is one that would have troubled Robert Frost. For him, the modernist poetry of Eliot and Pound, according to Robert Bernard Hass in *Going by Contraries: Robert Frost's conflict with science*, was an unconvincing riposte to science's post-Darwinian supremacy. Hass reads Frost's most famous poem. "The Road Not Taken" in the light of the poet's vexed relationship with science – as "a poetic declaration of independence from a society that values utility more than it does aesthetics".

For David Morley, much more springs from the common ground between art and science than Frosty philosophical conflict and *A Quark for Mister Mark*, Maurice Riordan and Jon Turney's anthology of 101 poems about science. There is certainly no evidence here of a "Two Cultures"-style debate that posits a petulant and etymologically unsound rivalry between art and science. Nor is Morley's project a straightforward attempt to reinvigorate the poetic lexicon with cadenced equations or unlikely chemical neologisms. He merely treats the practices of science and poetry as "a single discussion" held in "the same laboratory of language":

> You must examine unsettled matters and relationships. Do not evade responsibility: you must discuss the implications of what you've done . . . Too often the significance of findings is not discussed or not discussed well.

The epigraph by Mandelstam comes from his essay "On the Naturalists"; written in 1932 near the time of the poet's exile to the European Russian city of Voronezh. Several of the poems that follow take their cue (a line, an image, or an idea) from Mandelstam (who chose to serve his sentence in Voronezh on the advice of a biologist acquaintance): "Darwin's compositional method is the serial development of signs . . . Imagine a scholar-gardener leading guests around his estate, stopping among the flowerbeds to offer explanations; or an amateur zoologist welcoming his good friends in a zoological garden".

There are also purely practical resemblances: as the first of Morley's fifty "papers" declares (and this is the first book in a projected trilogy): "Without publication science is dead". The fiftieth consists of a quotation from Albert Einstein, seemingly set as verse:

> Where the world ceases to be the scene
> of our personal hopes and wishes, where we face it
> as free beings admiring, asking and observing, there we enter the realm of art and science.

As a practitioner of both kinds of literature, and a teacher of both scientific and creative writing at Warwick University, Morley is well placed to judge of such matters. The reader, in turn, should approach this book in the spirit of Mandelstam's scholar-gardener. Morley's specimens are best examined in strict order, however, and are not fit for haphazard buzzing. The concluding "Materials and Methods" are reassuringly short and, on the whole, not the difficult elucidations you might expect. So there is no cause for alarm; *Scientific Papers* consists almost exclusively of – would you believe it – aesthetically rewarding poems.

One of the first things that you notice about Morley's corner of this realm is its chilliness. From Romany encampments on the borders of society to deep seas, Kerensky's despondent days in the Winter Palace, and the call of Blackpool's wild bingo hall ("The Wakes"), the permafrost lies beneath:

On the blue, four and two.
On the white, your camera-light.
Blackpool queues, how do you do's.
Blackpool's wealth, the brain's on a shelf.
Knock it back. Bring it up.

But "The Wakes" is an atypical attempt at exuberant foot-stamping, not unlike Louis MacNeice's "Bagpipe Music". Elsewhere, Morley sounds closer to the 1930s Auden: "Low pressure over Voronezh. / The barometer held its breath". And again in "The Goodnight":

An owl unfolds across the bed:
its eyes, hungover can see the dead;
the swerving and the narrow hours
are no longer mine, no longer yours:
perfect ships of life and work
butt each other in the dark.

The poems in *Of Science* are anonymous, in homage to the *Lyrical Ballads*. This said, Morley follows the Romantic tradition further in *Scientific Papers* by reclaiming several of these poems as his own. They benefit greatly from being seen in sequence, forming the image of a life and history stretching out behind it, simultaneously defying and inviting accurate investigation. "Bamboo" beings with "trees [coming] out of their changing room in April / like green fighters, like players for a new season"; only halfway through does the narrator manifest himself as an "I", creeping through this spring crowd "to eye-spy what vexes him so". The next poem ("The Site") begins:

Why am I trailing you,
now through a pine-wood,
now through the words I write...?

Morley's enquiries produce numerous reasons to read this excellent book.

Churches of Rubble

SIMON COPPOCK

John Wilkinson, *Effigies Against the Light*
Salt, £9.95, ISBN 1876857382

IF YOU'VE NEVER read John Wilkinson's poetry, the best place to start in this collection of his 1990s work is *Sarn Helen* (1997). Begin at the beginning:

bayoneted. If any will hear the truth must cling best
avoid blow dragonflies, cling on by nail-feasance
over a cataract which scours a giant curtain wall,
or was it short-of-time shrunk the unseeming aimless
river to a bank's sediment?

What does it mean? Do you care what it means? If you do, I suggest it's because you find something intriguing about the brutal *in medias res* opening, about the malfeasance malapropism, about a familiar verbal signpost "If…" that points you nowhere, about the thumping rhythm that suddenly evaporates into sibilant alliterations.

Perhaps I should have started by quoting something more straightforward. This is "Skating to a Halt" from *Torn Off a Strip* (1994):

> Substitute for the hated tongues,
> steel ornithology,
>> for the webbed marshes,
> tracks of rubber.
>
> Substitute for the fierce lingo,
> spirit of plums,
>> for the nauseous cookery,
> food they'll never forget.
>
> Substitute for the wordy thicket,
> churches of rubble,
>> for songs in the orchard,
> kinsfolk in khaki.
>
> Substitute for the scolding girl,
> a belt, a haltered tree,
>> for the shifty-eyed,
> a stare they'll respect forever.

The repetitions and rhymes immediately mark this poem as more conventional than Sarn Helen, and there's even a sustained subject: this section of *Effigies* is (in part) concerned with the Bosnian conflict of the mid-1990s. Thus "steel ornithology" is a metaphor for bomber aircraft, "spirit of plums" is slivovitz (the region's plum brandy) and so on. What then of "the nauseous cookery"? Taking "nauseous" to mean nauseating rather than nauseated (I take the ambiguity to be deliberate, though I think it's unfortunate), the substitution of "nauseous cookery" for *better* food is unexpected; the prevailing rhetorical structure seems in the other stanzas to demand the better be replaced by the worse. There's also the odd diction: "ornithology" is at worst only a neutral term for the presumably genocidal bombing missions in the first stanza; "wordy thicket" is an accurate, but hardly positive, description of the peace negotiations in the third stanza. Thus it becomes clear that this is not a polemical list of the depredations of nationalist warmongers, but rather a careful balancing of descriptions of action – some banal, some brutal. There's the extirpation of an ethnic group, counterposed to the reinforcement of national identity by the national drink; the apparently idyllic "songs in the orchard" becoming militaristic "kinsfolk in khaki'; the last stanza's folk ritual in which the "haltered tree" takes punishment due to "the scolding girl"; and, finally, the substitution of "a stare" for "shifty-eyed". This last verbally enacts an improvement (the unwavering gaze – "stare" – replaces the wandering gaze – "shifty-eyed"), but the lines actually state that the stare is turned on the shifty-eyed who thus remain the victims. The key point is that Wilkinson uses a process of fine linguistic shading that obliges any reader giving the poem sufficient attention to make ethical discriminations that the poem itself refuses to make.

Effigies Against the Light is not a passive read. It is rather a densely written and combative book. "Abruptly a precise channel clips when he rocks steady", Wilkinson writes in *Sarn Helen*, Section 5. Even if "rocks steady" is recognized as a type of reggae, even if it is known that "channel clips" occur when the volume of an input channel peaks too high and distorts during recording, there seems to be no inside of this line to unpack. Clips (in the colloquial sense of "clips along") links with "Abruptly", thus connecting to both ends of the line, but while this knits literal, metaphorical, vernacular and specialist discourses tightly together, the meaning of the line remains irresolvable. Similarly, in Section 7:

> wreathed by image aspirations swirling from his lips,
> where's the metrical lesion, clip, the moment gold,
> the next manila & mnemosyne?

is held together by the sound patterning, more than the sense, which remains elusive. The poem seems to snap in and out of focus as each line is read, the shifts of focus often sparking explosions of sudden beauty or elusive signification: perhaps "the Christmas tree of a far refinery / burns off waste production makes an angel dance at the tip" ("Facing Port Talbot"), "reaching the far with stars on our arms" ("The Little One Has Its Day") or "The slow bubbles unfist" (*Sarn Helen*). Yet these pleasures remain – by their nature – superficial, modified from moment to moment as the reader passes by. Wilkinson has discussed the use of such non-technique or blank surface in relation to John Wieners' poetry (which he researched at Harvard in the 1970s). Wilkinson was deeply touched by the poet's diligently self-protected writing style: he felt the poet's very real mental vulnerability could be discerned in his avoidance rather than indulgence of excessive emotion. For me, though, the parts of *Effigies* (say the untitled section or "Happenstance" from *Reverses*, 1999) that most closely follow Wieners' hyperactively self-conscious writing style (lines like "subjects scrutiny opposite panic") were the very places where the writing was so purely virtuoso in its evasions that I lost all interest in the hunt.

Effigies collects four of Wilkinson's small-press publications and sundry fugitive pieces, with fugitive here being more a matter of presentation than accessibility: you aren't going to lay hands on the originals of any of these outside the small network of specialist poetry bookshops and certain major national or university libraries. Wilkinson has now been publishing poems for nearly three decades, and *Effigies* completes a trilogy of collections that span almost the whole of Wilkinson's writing career: *Oort's Cloud* (Barque Press, 1999) covers 1970–84 and *Flung Clear* (Parataxis, 1994) covers 1988–92, at which point *Effigies* takes over (puzzlingly, neither *Oort's Cloud* nor *Flung Clear* republish *Clinical Notes*, 1980, or *Proud Flesh*, 1986). It is also, in some ways, a shame that Salt chose to collect the most recent period of Wilkinson's activities. While many will be grateful (particularly for a reprint of the three Equipage pamphlets included), newcomers might have preferred a judicious selection. Indeed, *Oort's Cloud* would be the best starting point for Wilkinson's formidable *oeuvre*, running from his precocious – and often more inviting – early poems to his hard-won but sometimes breathtaking recent work.

Laughing All the Way

SIÂN HUGHES

Carol Ann Duffy, *Feminine Gospels*
Picador, £12.99, ISBN 03304886438
Carol Rumens, *Hex*
Bloodaxe, £7.95, ISBN 1852246022
Maura Dooley, *Sound Barrier: Poems 1982 – 2002*
Bloodaxe, £8.95, ISBN 1852245786

THE LAUGHTER OF the girl who starts the giggling on page one of the twenty-page "The Laughter of Stafford Girl's High"

> was a liquid one, a gurgle, a ripple, a dribble,
> A babble, a gargle, a plash, a splash of a laugh
> Like the sudden jackpot leap of a silver fish
> In the purse of a pool.

In prose one would have to go for the best word, ditch the rest, and get on with the story. The trouble is, after a page or ten, my brain slips ineluctably over into novel-reader mode; I want to be involved in the story, interested in the characters, and I don't want eighteen words for the same thing, even if they entertainingly almost half rhyme. In a way, this kind of incantatory list-making is the very opposite of the contemporary list poem: more than anything it resembles the very traditional art of rhetoric, persuasive speech-making. Duffy's fluent speech-maker uses repetition, simple question-and-answer stuff – "What was she queen of?" "What were her laws?" – and can slide from one image to another without need of plot (the "long queen" starts off as Elizabeth I, and returns to her later, when she sends her explorers out, but this does not stop her also being invisible, Rapunzel, the fairy-tale judge who visits in the guise of an old woman, and a few other things beside). The danger of this kind of fluency is that it writes itself into a knot: "and was queen of more, of all the dead / when they lived if they did so female." Despite the subject matter, childbirth, moons and menstruation, and the kind of crib-gazing I can't help feeling one should keep to oneself, this strikes me as a peculiarly masculine form of verse. This is poetry of ideas, and it needs a conceit strong and flexible enough to hold it together. There are occasions when this happens: in "Sub" the central image of a female substitute who stepped into every famous (and therefore male) sporting moment is a rich one, and there is plenty of excellent material to keep it moving along. "The Map Woman", whose skin grows a map of her home town is a central image powerful and inventive enough on which to pin a longish poem. The best moment of the book, however, is the sonnet "Wish" – where the fluency serves a simple purpose simply and well. Here the similes are mundane for good reason – "her shroud like washing / blown onto the grass" – while the trademark echoes stress the words worth dwelling on – "Nobody died. Nobody / wept. Nobody slept who couldn't be woken".

The success of Carol Rumens's *Hex* is that individual poems are far more interesting than the political idea behind them, and far richer and more various than a series of protest songs. The poetry is densely peopled, clamorous with voices, tender, furious, and cut with an edge of hilarious clarity. "Kings of the Playground" is one of the many poems that cry out to be read aloud – full of bitter jokes and childlike repetition:

> Bully TV was launched. There was only one programme
> "How We Bashed the Bully". Anyone who switched off
> was sentenced to 25 years community-bullying.
> The Bully-Bashers relaxed. Gave themselves medals. Flew home.

The meaning of "bully" shifts from stanza to stanza, slippery as news-speak, inevitable as the terrible logic of the final declarations "Three cheers for old Bully!" and "Make way for Old Bully, ya cunts!" Equally memorable for its form and imagery, the brilliant, "Rigor Mortis" is surely one of the best war poems of its age, its elegant dance of repeated lines framed by the first and last – "Someone should tell them they're dead". The poem's diction is simple, and so the revolving form never upstages the central image: two dead soldiers facing each other across a bridge. But there is no loss of interest. Where Duffy's prolixity tends to impede the narrative, Rumens's simplicity achieves all the elegance and forward motion of good prose. In a similarly clipped and memorable tone, "Just as in 1914" uses repeated lines to illustrate the timelessness of its message – "You can sell the young".

But the overall tone of the collection is far more colourful and compulsive than these rhetorically restrained poems suggest. The almost-title poem, "The Quest, The Hex, the Alkahest" is the roller-coaster spiked history of a Jekyll-and-Hyde creator/destroyer stirring hate into the human brew from day one –

> Your favourites walked the plank
> in front of you. I had you hexed,
>
> hoaxed, on fire, hung from a spike,
> gnawed out by cancers,
>
> wild-eyed with Alzheimer's,
> laid low by machete attack.

What Rumens' voices have in common is the bravado, the assurance, of the beautiful-but-damned: whether it is Sylvia Plath taking a swipe from beyond the grave, the voice of a "rogue translator" taking liberties with the unsaid, or the un-creator wishing a philo-sophically fond farewell to the un-engendered along with the undone:

> Darlings, you can't all have names:
> we've got hearts, we've got favourites.
> Some of you are top of our pops;
> a few are on the tip of our tongues,
> but some (that's life) are not.

Compared to the theatricals that characterise the work of both these women writers, the work of Maura Dooley seems to perform a delicate balance. Rather than the rhetoric of public speaking, the voice is intimate, understated, deliberately prosaic. Nonetheless, the central concern of the verse is to hold the external, political world against an internal personal monologue. Reading a retrospective like this is fascinating: as well as a history of how the poet's craft has been honed and refined, it is a history of the political concerns of the years charted by her work from 1982 to 2002. From *Ivy Leaves and Arrows* (1982) there are "Questions You Can't Answer" – questions about the earth, the way it is divided, about bloodshed and how to keep your hands clean, about whether or not to eat South African oranges. In *Turbulence* in 1988 there are "Missiles Over Buxton", nightmare shadows under the bed that surface in the news over breakfast in "Banging the Bomb", and some of the first instances of where the poet's voice hits and holds the note that will achieve its trademark tightrope-tension of personal/political. From "Shadow on Her Desk" –

> Don't play outside today (I'm crying).
> Wash all green-leaved vegetables thoroughly.
> Don't drink rainwater (I'm crying).
>
> Saddleworth, Aberfan, Chernobyl: a kind of litany.
> Up on the wet green moor police start to dig.

By *Explaining Magnetism* (1991), the life of the city and the life of the mind have become so metaphorically enmeshed it is no longer possible to say which is the subject, which is the subtext. This is where it starts to get seriously interesting, the quashed prose refusing to weigh heavily on either side of the equation, the perfectly uninsistent voice conjuring a life of our times from tiny detail:

> The streets yield up their dead
> Alive, loused up, leaky,
>
> Dancing till dawn
> In ball-gowns or rags;

Refugee nannies weep over the intercom, "Other people's sadnesses / blow in like dust", and the beauty of it is, it sounds so simple, that a cool and sympathetic gaze can rest on human history, that a clear voice can attempt to pitch some consolation against it. In "A Visit to the Optician" from the section of new poems, the poet asks for clarity of vision, staking a claim not to the martyrdom of a visionary, nor the inward-turning vision of a martyr to any of the common causes, but something that aims to be almost scientific, the strength of purpose to bear witness:

> I'm not Saint Lucy, who tore out her eyes
> the better to see. I will not be blinded by love,
> you, the delusions of my age. Lend me some glasses.
> Pass the telescope. I'll stuff these lenses in.
> I will not miss the passing of this heavenly body.

Snip the Blind Jeremy

ROBERT SAXTON

John Hartley Williams, *Spending Time with Walter*
Cape, £8.00, ISBN 0224061763
Ruth Padel, *Voodoo Shop*
Chatto, £8.99, ISBN 0701173017
Paul Farley, *The Ice Age*
Picador, £7.99, ISBN 0330484532

REPEATEDLY LAUNCHING HIMSELF beyond the limits of the given, John Hartley Williams engenders strange new worlds, all the more unsettling for their resemblances to the world we inhabit. *Spending Time with Walter* is a book of vivid narratives riddled with inversions, squirming with discomforts and driven by a compelling logic very much the poet's own: a logic you might call "dreamlike", except that its scenarios are so fully present to all the senses. Each poem is like a little movie by Buñuel, but one that captures smell and touch as convincingly as sight and sound.

In "Dog", a nocturnal canine elegy, the poet yearns for another planet where the dross of the "ruined earth" is alchemized into joy. Grief gives "the once-clean darkness of water . . . a covering of scum" – and in the parallel dimension the poet craves, Scum becomes the resurrected dog's new name, as if some law of nature requires hopelessness to survive vestigially even in Elysium. The poem ends with absolute darkness falling as the dog-owner kneels to welcome his bounding, panting pet in a moment of annihilating transcendence.

One thing that fascinates Williams is imperfect machinery, which takes on comically surreal attributes even when clanking away in a naturalistic setting. "You Deal with the Noises" describes an emergency visit by a plumber or heating engineer who works in the basement while the household busies itself with chores or ablutions. "You unpack your slunth caliper, and set it up, / affix two trivets / and start the slambolica." Then comes the offbeat climax: "Like someone who's discovered anguish, / you snip the blind Jeremy". The irritating slunth noises cease, whereupon the workman lets himself out, his selfless heroism unappreciated: "Sometimes they're in the bathroom, splashing noisily: / *the back door's open*, they call". Akin to this, but more elaborate in its invention, is "The Machine", which tells of an "Engine of Good Fortune" devised by a Frenchman, Jacques Le Sourd, on commission for a Herefordshire farmer's orchard in the late 19th century. Again the environment of the poem is recognizable, yet alongside the central conceit of the generator any small incidental opportunity for fantasy is gleefully prized open – even the name of a comet ("Mavis Doolittle's comet") and the flowers whose scent fills the evening (I-Forget-the- Name, Ripefrock, Odorendrum).

Such Mannerist high jinks are characteristic of Williams, but sometimes a deeper note of complex, unsayable feeling cuts across them. Here is a moment, in "The View from Bird Rock", after the sea-watchers have fruitlessly scanned the waters for dolphins:

> The ocean boomed. We seemed
> to hear demonic deep fidelity
> being sworn in language
> not by any means describable in ours.

In *Voodoo Shop*, Ruth Padel's poems travel: across the globe, through the years, between generations, crossing frontiers between inner and outer realms, even between the human and the cosmic. Powering many of them is a reflex of reminscence, which never becomes nostalgia. Her realism about love is twice bitten, never shy – well versed in endings, she'd always be game, one feels, to start again, differently. By remembering, she keeps what is valuable as close as can be – which is never as close as happy families, perhaps because there's no such thing. Our identity is the sum of all our relationships, all our moments of being together and apart.

Padel's writing is often described as sexy, but in this volume at least she seldom lingers on the body. There are two brief filmic acts of lovemaking, one on a kitchen table, the other on a pebbly beach. There is also a passionate letter to Eugene Onegin, "after Pushkin". Always, though, sensual overtones play abundantly around the poet's radar, alert to everything from "rowdy ripples of cranberry vinegar" in a delicatessen window to the "soft sapphire dusk" on Copacabana Beach where boys play "manic soccer . . . To an audience of rearing, floodlit, diamond surf". And there are intimacies on every page. In "A Lick and a Promise", Padel brings us right into the lovers' bathroom to show us a shaving stick, with its "heartline-friendly handle" and its splay of bristles that

> polar-bear your cheekbones every morning.
> Abandoned on our New
> York basin's luxury mauve lip
>
> As if you'd gone to Washington for a day,
> A week, a year, and when you're back
> Might kiss me through
> Fine flowing handlebars. A Father Christmas leer.

Typical here are the fleeting irony of "luxury", the restless shifting through gears of time, the "year" / "leer" slant-rhyme half-found, half-made, and the anticipated homecoming which manages to be, at once, wittily surreal and embarrassingly plausible.

The last poem in the collection, "Casablanca and the Children of the Storm", is a *tour de force* in which Padel shows just how wildly digressive she can be without for a moment losing her grip on the main theme, the end of a six-year affair, which in the closing lines is beautifully assayed as an alloy of "magnetism" and "faith". Nor is love her only subject. She is also a moving elegist. Padel shows us palpably that sexual love and familial grief spring from the same psychic soil.

Paul Farley's first collection, *The Boy from the Chemist is Here to See You* (1998), contained, among a handful of outstanding poems, two favourites of mine: "Laws of Gravity" and "Treacle". Farley's second book, *The Ice Age*, takes his concern with the mental and emotional residues of childhood into a bleaker register, without any sacrifice of wit. Here the poet seems far from comfortable with the rockpools left within his inner landscape by retreating tides of time. Initially we might wonder why. In the book's first poem his melancholy seems existential: why should he feel, as he rumbles through England on a train, gazing out of the window, that "months of Sunday school" and "gallons of free milk" have made him "a single fool / reflected endlessly on the night air"? By the time we reach the last poem, however, describing an imaginary journey to an island off the coast of Iceland, with a coda that returns him to his Liverpool childhood, "old / beyond my years in the youngest place on earth", we have got to know him better.

Highlights of *The Ice Age* are "11th February 1963", an abbreviated elegy in which the suicide of Sylvia Plath mysteriously prefigures the assassination of John Lennon; "Winter Hill", the occasion of which is imperfect TV reception in the Pennines; "Diary Moon", with its Larkinesque high-windowed view of one generation succeeding another; "Umbrella", a disquisition on the curiously heartfelt relationship we can have with a manufactured object; and "Negatives", which reminds us, like so many of these poems, of what we might otherwise have forgotten we knew – among the darks made light and the lights made dark, "the middle key / we sometimes find unchanged".

Out of This World

ANDREA BRADY

Peter Robinson, *Poetry, Poets, Readers: Making Things Happen*
Oxford University Press, £40, ISBN 0199251134

WITHOUT SAYING SO directly, Peter Robinson's new essays repeatedly engage with Philip Sidney's *Defence of Poesie*. Poetry's relegation to "another world", the caveat that the poet "nothing affirmeth, and therefore never lieth", the poet's authority as *vates*, the difference between human and animals being the ability to promise (or *oratio* and *ratio*), the arguable supremacy of poetry or philosophy – all these themes find prompts in the *Defence*. But where Sidney's own poetics were bolstered by a humanist idealism about the efficacy of verse in public life, *Poetry, Poets, Readers* avoids such clearly drawn vectors of reading and consequence.

Rejecting Auden's defeatist dictum that "poetry makes nothing happen", Robinson sets out to discover what poetry *does* make happen, and how. Rather than citing practical or material consequences of verse production, he uses linguistic philosophy to define categorically how poetry operates on readers. The conviction, pleasures and gratitude of committed reading are evident in his affirmation of the poetic contract between readers and writers. Nonetheless, these essays finally deliver another version of the limited efficacy he sets out to critique.

Robinson begins by considering Auden's prognostication within the context of the poet's own changing political ideology. He goes on to discuss the kind of information poetry can or cannot be expected to give, applying the fact/value distinction to poetry and focusing on those questions which readers suspend in order to enjoy reading verse. Next, in a corrective reading of Helen Vendler, he resituates Shakespeare's sonnets in the social and economic transactions which they were intended actually to negotiate. In a final chapter, he criticises Paul Muldoon's poetry for using humour to remove itself to a "secondary world" that trivialises the importance of political events. The book ends with a kind of tribute to the stay-at-home poetry reader: since poetry demonstrably *does* make things happen in history, Robinson concludes, this effectiveness must arise from how it makes things happen on daily basis in individual readings.

Wittgenstein, J. L. Austin, and John Searle provide the theoretical groundwork for these meditations. Robinson bravely defines poems: they are informal institutional facts, brought into existence by performative (promissory) utterances, which require institutional backing and yet lack the official or legal status accorded by formal institutions. They promise truthfulness, accuracy, perpetuity, and generosity, pledges which Robinson seeks to repay with the faithfulness of his own readings.

As an unofficial institutional fact, he says, poetry lacks the institutional power of enforcement. Its "tokens . . . do not have officially-sanctioned authority to perform or facilitate direct actions upon the materials of the world". Only by the "tokens" of its status does poetry acquire a kind of institutionality. Thus, Robinson argues, poetry affects "readers' lives" through an act of pretence. "People wouldn't read poetry if it didn't do *something* for them. This is its function or use in a life. It does this thing because, in Auden's phrase, it is 'a way of happening', and because it has thus made something happen for the reader, so it can have an influence on the life of the reader, contributing to some material change, small or large, in the history of man." Confusingly, he seems to be explaining that people read poems because poetry functions to make things happen because it is a way of making things happen because it does make things happen for readers. And, particularly, does "something for them". What that something is, Robinson is kept from saying by his interest in a broadly categorical definition of how poetry works. It could be a kind of rapturous transport, a bemused smile of self-recognition, a cognisance of truth; *Poetry, Poets, Readers* tends to focus on such reactions of pleasurable consumption and self-enrichment rather than any more explicitly public or political action.

Nodding to Plato and Sidney, Robinson acknowledges that pretending is part of the definition of how poetry works. The reader is able "simultaneously to respond to the text in two distinct ways: *as if* these were real speech acts, and in the knowledge that they are not". But for Sidney, poetry's ability to fabricate worlds was the source of its transformative potential. A capacity of imagining a different world showed the instrumental potency of human reason in changing this one. Consigning poetry to a "secondary world" can only be pejorative if the act of ethical creation involved is derided or this world is considered good enough. I'd suggest that few poets committed to experimental and rigorous language use, together with the aim of revolutionising society and human interactions through and in art, would agree with Robinson that poetry is primarily an art of "pretending".

But in this way, Robinson's conclusions seem to suffer from the poverty of his sample. He writes that "poets so often choose to end their poems not with the direct expressions of feeling but the performance of some action that may deliver the feeling but doesn't directly express it. Poets rightly go in fear of such assertions unsupported by contexts of action and exchange". That moralizing word "rightly" indicates Robinson's own predilection for *praxis* (art, skill) over *gnosis* (knowledge, recognition). But he is also generalising about a poetic technique which might only apply to certain producers of occasional verse – Auden, Yeats, Elizabeth Bishop, John Matthias, Joseph Brodsky, Heaney, Muldoon, Philip Larkin. Consequently, the abstracted inclusiveness of Robinson's definitions is derived from readings of particularly personalist, occasional poets.

Robinson is convincing in his rejection of Auden's preposterous statement that "if not a poem had been written, not a picture changed, not a bar of music composed, the history of man would be materially unchanged". But as examples of poetry changing human history, he offers: the effect of Shakespeare's works on English idiom; the effect of the Sistine Ceiling on Italy's and the Vatican's tourist economies; the fervour and xenophobia generated by national anthems played at football matches. From Milton to Mayakovsky, the most radical or revolutionary examples are ignored; so is Marxist criticism of art and commitment. Robinson's argument therefore seems artificially and problematically limited. His assertion (about Muldoon's poetry on the Irish Troubles) that "the making things happen that poems achieve involves a far more subtle and long-lasting realignment of human minds and bodies than any such outrages from one side of a border or another" could, I think, be challenged by literary history.

Disappointingly, Robinson's discussion of pre-modern writing is often limited and tokenistic. Where Robinson does take up writers who flourished before the 20th century, significant opportunities to refine his description of the "institutional" status of poetry are missed. It would help, for example, to note the context of Cowley's reluctance to include any of his juvenile *Poetical Blossomes* in his 1668 *Works*. Cowley's wasted "promise" also implicated the Stuarts' unfulfilled promises to reward his loyalty. Robinson makes a vague comment about Cowley demonstrating "that the promissory nature of poems requires the collaboration of circumstances both at the times of production and reception". But the preface which mentions the unfinished *Civil War* was first published in Cowley's 1656 *Poems*, not in 1668. That year, Cowley had just returned from exile in France, where he was employed as an emissary and personal correspondent for Henrietta Maria. Arrested and on bail until the Restoration, Cowley wrote the preface when his own writerly labour, and his freedom of expression and movement, were actually curtailed by formal institutional facts. His criticisms of his own Royalist party in that same preface might have contributed to his unsuccessful applications for sinecures in 1661; certainly, Cowley often used verse to complain about his neglect by the royal family after his faithful service to it as a writer.

Similarly, Edmund Waller's "Of English Verse" is cited from a Penguin anthology as proof that Waller, who hopes he will be read in the future, still is. However, Waller's poem bemoans the consequences of readers' own language use on the possibility of perpetuity. He tells poets to write in Greek or Latin, since English – as a living tongue – changes, making old usages like Chaucer's incomprehensible. Here, Waller's well-known antipathy toward innovation ought to be placed in the context of his own political career. An MP from the age of sixteen, Waller was himself imprisoned for plotting to hand the City of London over to the King. That his eloquence saved him from execution, and his panegyrics and personal wit redeemed him from the disgrace of his confessions, seem relevant to the way Waller's poetry made things happen.

Both Waller and Cowley wrote elaborate panegyrics that contributed to the effusion of relief, bounty and hopefulness at the Restoration, which in turn produced a climate for national reconciliation, indemnity and toleration. Both fulfilled conspicuously official functions; and both offer interesting examples of how poets, through their interactions with official institutions, prove a semi-official status is never far from any writer. For these reasons, they might contravene Robinson's odd assertion that the statement "Rosetti is a poet" entails no institutional status and authority because poets don't sit exams or, for the most part, get elected or get governmental pay.

Robinson's review of Vendler's *The Art of Shakespeare's Sonnets* widens his historical frame of reference. And his criticisms of Vendler's imprecise usage of the term "speech act" shows how meticulous is his own application of Searle's and Austin's philosophies. His worthwhile rejection of Vendler's New Critical paradigms is complicated, however, by Robinson's own celebration of the immeasurably personal and unspecific effects of poetry on readers' lives. He doesn't ask enough questions, in part out of a misplaced sense of decorum. He explains that "The purpose of such delicacy in the questioning of texts is to keep them in human history while at the same time granting them their character as art – as life in art and art in life", adding that "they have to be granted their character as art, and questioned accordingly, so that they can, in their own way, act, and they have to be understood as operating within the continuum of history for this acting to be on something, on ordinary human lives". So poetry becomes a purposive speech act, whose only purpose is its own incalculable effects on the ethos of a private reading. But surely some questions may be relevantly tendentious, and it is the failure of a particular subset of modernist occasional poetry that it makes such questions – often the most important, if also the most abrasive – seem impolite.

Do You Know Who We Are?

PETER MCDONALD

Shira Wolosky, *The Art of Poetry: How to Read a Poem*
Oxford University Press USA, £17.99, ISBN 0195138708
Ruth Padel, *52 Ways of Looking at a Poem:*
Or How Reading Modern Poetry Can Change Your Life
Chatto, £12.99, ISBN 0701173181

LEARNING HOW TO read poetry, like learning how to write it, is not something that happens of its own accord. At some point or other, advice and guidance are needed; what's needed, too, is information to help an initial impulse or facility develop. A superstition has taken hold – in Britain at least – that giving information is somehow offensive or offputting, that it has to be tempered with the right attitude or affiliation, as sympathetic outreach. A worrying consequence of this is the transformation of educational writing about poetry into a PR job *for* poetry: and then, inevitably, into a sales-pitch for a small band of con- temporary poets. The reading public, whose intelligence ought to be respected, quite rightly feel suspicious about much contemporary poetry, partly because of the blatant nonsense, and equally obvious nepotism, which show themselves time and again in the way that poetry is promoted.

However constricted their taste, or conservative their inclinations, public attitudes to poetry are certainly correct in one respect: poetry's essence is not in its immediacy, chattiness, or lifestyle-value, but in its formal power and memorability. This means, at the most superficial level, that poetry of the past looks better, on the whole, than much poetry of the present. To regard such a view as either ignorant or outmoded is to engage in precisely that "elitism" which many promoters of contemporary poetry are at such pains to condemn.

In teaching poetry, the place to start is form: and poetic form is a subject that opens out to the most complicated, and important, issues of language, audience, and meaning. Any good educational text will enable its readers to see these issues clearly: explaining poetic form is not a process of facile demystification ("look, here's how it's all done…"), but of showing a way into the mystery itself. As most committed readers of poetry know, and as new readers soon find out, it pays to be a little wary of people eager to press upon us their own definitions of poetry. And yet, in order to explain poetry, or to encourage others to begin that long process of explanation for themselves, some kinds of preliminary definition are almost unavoidable. Shira Wolosky's *The Art of Poetry* starts with a useful enough definition, claiming the poem as "a dynamic arena in which elements from outside as well as inside collide and reassemble". That will do: at least, it is a point from which intelligent discussion can begin, and it sets the terms for thinking seriously about what is "outside" and "inside" poetic frames, as well as the complicated question of the place of audiences there. Wolosky builds well on these points, writing that the poem is "a self-conscious site, a field in which the operations of language become visible", thus offering us "a strange and marvellous mirror for seeing how language itself works in shaping our world".

Wolosky is not in the business of "selling" poetry, but of educating readers who (we can safely suppose) are willing to be educated. *The Art of Poetry: How to read a poem* is published in the USA, and this may have something to do with its sense of intellectual confidence: the author never lets any element of self-doubt show through in the development of an educative project. Although everybody will have quibbles about particular readings here, and about degrees of emphasis given to different things, the project itself is both coherent and concise, relying on close readings of short, post-medieval poems (with some twentieth-century but no contemporary work) to introduce concepts of diction, syntax, metre, and rhyme. At its best, the book shows that clarity of discussion need not sell short depth of analysis, or complexity of awareness, and it is an excellent starting-point for any serious consideration of form in poetry, of what poetry does to language and what language is always ready to do to poetry. In other words, it's an academic book in the best sense.

All of this, however, suffers badly in translation from American to British literary culture, where learning about poetry can no longer be presented upfront as an academic activity (since "academic" is by now almost a routine slur), and seems to have become instead a part of the self-help industry. Ruth Padel's clarion call at the start of her book is indicative of a great deal:

> We are in the middle of a large-scale renaissance of poetry in Britain today. It began in the late seventies and is still going strong. Never, even in the most glamorous eras of English poetry, like the Elizabethan or Victorian, have so many published poets been developing new ways of saying things to people in so many different parts of society.

One question that immediately arises is, *Can this be true?* Another – and a more interesting one – is, *Why are you talking to us like this?* As far as the first is concerned, I can only respond that no, I really don't think contemporary British poetry measures up to the inflated claims Padel is making for it, and certainly not on the basis of some of the "published poets" reprinted in her book. But answering the second question is a longer – and a more revealing – business.

52 Ways of Looking At A Poem collects Ruth Padel's columns from *The Independent on Sunday*, in which she reprinted a contemporary poem each week, and gave a commentary on its workings. The feature was a successful one, at least for a while (until "a new editor arrived who did not fancy 'all that writing under the poem'"), and, on the evidence of this volume, Padel remains mightily impressed by the scale of her own success. But "success" is a complicated term. In a book which sets out to explain "How reading modern poetry can change your life", it seems odd to encounter so much discussion of the courage required to commission the feature, and so much celebration of the public demand for the column, alongside lengthy digressions on the iniquities of British journalism and the shortcomings of newspaper books pages. In fact, despite the cringe-making subtitle, we are never told how exactly our lives can be changed by reading modern poetry, though Padel implies often enough that modern poets can have their lives changed for the better by our reading (and buying) their work. It quickly becomes apparent that British poets have a tough time breaking into the world of the media, and that all this is somebody else's fault.

Certain basic assumptions go completely unaddressed: why, for example, does it matter that poets should have regular press outlets? Why, indeed, should anyone who wants poetry (or

> If a reader wants to learn things, then he or she has a right to be taught them, without introductory offers, the soft politics of life-style marketing, messages from the sponsor, or false promises.

anything) to change their life be bothered by the fact that "poetry has never had such a low profile in the media"? And how on earth are new readers to be won over to contemporary poetry when this introduction spends so much energy on complaining about the unfairness of the literary world? "None of this is complaint", Padel protests at one point, "It is reportage"; but that term, "reportage", redolent of all kinds of hack culture, seems damagingly unselfconscious.

So, why *does* Padel, an intelligent writer, choose to write like this? What is at issue here is the relation between poetry and the language of education, and our confidence in using such language. Shira Wolosky writes that "poetry's forms are not fixed abstractions … Rather, they give design to that moment of encounter between writer and audience, within terms of expectation and mutual positioning, and within a larger social organization that frames them both". This bears thinking about, but it does take time to consider. Compare it with Padel on poetic form: "In my newspaper discussions", she writes, "I did not use many technical terms but talked mainly about echoes and sound-relationships. For that's where it's really at. What makes 'a poem' is not rhyme itself, but hanging together". As to what "hanging together" means, Padel seems to intend the rhymes, and the chains of vowel-repetition, or consonantal alliteration, which can be identified in a given poem. But this ignores completely the extra dimension insisted upon in Wolosky's formulation, which links "design" to "encounter", form to expectation. For Padel, a poem works according to a miraculously internal and self-contained logic, the "craft", as she calls it, which identifies it as something special, addressing the world of "ordinary people", but sealed off from their objections; for Wolosky (as for many critics, in fact), that self-containment is an illusion, or only one part of the truth, since poetic form, like language itself, is part of a complex, and changing, reality beyond the individual poet. No good poet has ever enjoyed the absolute confidence about his or her control of language and form which Padel seems to take for granted. This, in fact, is "where it's really at"; but Padel either can't see it, or feels that it's an idea she can't sell to the newspapers.

It seems to be axiomatic, in Padel's world, that readers shouldn't be intellectually challenged (poems, she reassures us, are as easy to "read", with practice, as movies or TV ads); at the same time, the actual reading public is chided for its failure to see the poetry renaissance going on in its midst. There is a great deal of complacency in this, and perhaps finally a condescending attitude towards the "audience" whose attention Padel so much covets. "Changes in education", we are assured, "mean that people know different things",

and Padel unembarrassedly sees this as proof of an advance on the past, with the spurious reasoning that "the variety of poetry available in Britain reflects the ethnic, educational and regional variety of the people writing it". If this sounds like advertising copy for a supermarket's new line in fruit and veg, that is because Padel has chosen to use exactly the register of promotion and product-spin which, she believes, calls the media shots. So, her lengthy introductory essay leaves no buzzword untouched: it speaks – without any irony whatsoever – the language of the sales-pitch and the PR exercise, eagerly miming along to the excited tones of a "culture" industry. When she calls the media "the mirror of our culture", Padel lets all this show; and never – not for an instant – does she pause to wonder what might be implicit in that "our". This unselfconsciousness about language is not another sign of how far we have all advanced in terms of education – on the contrary: but it is a vital indicator of how seriously a writer takes the business of writing. It is matched neatly in Jo Shapcott's jacket blurb for the book, where she hails Padel's introduction as something "that will come to be seen as the summary description of the age … a description of where and who we are". Well, yes, I think it will: though "we" is a group to which fewer belong, or want to belong, than Padel and Shapcott might imagine.

There is something offensive about lamenting the public's lack of taste, especially when this turns out to mean a failure to appreciate the taste of the person issuing the lamentations. Padel is not alone in thinking that the reading public need to be addressed as though they were in a remedial class, or were in collective need of emotional therapy (see Neil Astley's definitive *Staying Alive* anthology), but she is notable for the frankness with which she puffs the poets in whom her "renaissance" consists. How does a poet get into Padel's club, this fabulous renaissance generation? First, some fuzzily political qualifications are required: in a bizarre account, Padel depicts the 1980s Ren. Gen. as "unsalaried, travelling to underpaid readings in unfunded poetry societies, teaching in increasingly run-down schools with plastic buckets put out to catch leaks from the roof", before claiming that "poems increasingly spoke of the inner effects of Thatcherism" – these "inner effects" including many bad things, from "extinction of animal species" to "a war played out on our own TV screens". (If these were the inner effects, what can the outward ones have been like?) Second, it's important to have some kind of identity to flog (regional, sexual, or ethnic), if you can't manage to be Irish – though a good many of Padel's chosen poets do, in fact, manage this. Third, you have to understand that "contemporary poetry ladles from all today's verbal puddles" and be committed to "raiding the pacey wit, irony and allusiveness of ads and the increasingly dominant media". Above all, however, you must not be elitist: "Whatever 'elitist' is, the poets in this book are not it … Not all went to college, few went to Oxbridge, none (not even the Nobel Prize-winners) are rich", Padel assures her readers, claiming finally that "There are a lot of acute, lively, and non-elitist minds out there making poems from the world we live in: from styles of thought and phrase, jokes, events and experiences we all share". It should be pointed out that Padel's complacent use of "elitist" here, like the cynical deployment of the term by politicians and journalists, shows nothing but a contempt for the "people" it pretends to value. In poetry, it's simply a meaningless term – Ben Jonson was "elitist", Milton and Tennyson were "elitist": get over it.

Padel is, of course, writing in a newspaper register, and her disposable jargon is there for effect; it cannot function to educate readers, but tries to tell them what they want, by reminding them of who they want to be. But like the politicians, Padel is vulnerable in so far as she underestimates the intelligence of "people"; and "people", I would suggest, will not take kindly to being assured of poetry's "non-elitist" properties by someone so confident that the world she lives in is the one "we live in". Remarking on how far we have come from T. S. Eliot and Ezra Pound, Padel notes how "cultural changes" have meant that today's poets "have a totally different relation to their readers", since "The only cultural knowledge they are sure to have in common with them is television and its realist counterpart, the street". Padel's whole enterprise, with its low view of "cultural knowledge", and its reductive (and – at book length – drearily repetitious) insistence on one very limited conception of poetic "craft", becomes a kind of manifesto for the Ren. Gen.: origin and affiliation count for a lot, everybody is tremendously talented (just look at all the prizes they give each other), and if you don't appreciate it you're missing out on something enormously fashionable and "now". Whether Padel and her poets constitute a self-promoting "elite" is not a question raised in the book, but it might well occur to any reader who pays attention to the litany of praise and hyperbole contained there.

It's tempting to contrast all this with the respect for the reader which Shira Wolosky's introduction to poetry takes as a given in educational writing, and to see here a telling sign of the provincial nature of British "culture" in comparison with American practice. If a reader wants to learn things, then he or she has a right to be taught them, without introductory offers, the soft politics of life-style marketing, messages from the sponsor, or false promises. To foster a love of poetry, several things will always be necessary: belief and enthusiasm, certainly; but also a respect for the intelligence of those who, beginning as pupils, will become partners in the conversation that poems initiate, across time and place, as parts of a common and inexhaustible cultural resource. Like any conversation, this isn't a matter of some vaguely-conceived passive uplift, but of engagement and stimulation; and yes, it can sometimes be difficult, as we can all be difficult. Learning about poetry teaches us not to expect too much from ourselves and our own time, for good poetry has always been thin on the ground; it is in the nature of mediocrity, on the other hand, to be continually proclaiming its own renaissance.

Weather Channel

JUSTIN QUINN

Robert Minhinnick, *After the Hurricane*
Carcanet, £6.95, ISBN 185754563X

THE PUBLICATION OF Robert Minhinnick's *Selected Poems* in 1999 did not indicate that an important poet had been overlooked. Most of the poems were tight-lipped accounts of various realisations to do with landscapes and their inhabitants. If Minhinnick was different, it was in the way that he was able to erase his personality while still talking in the first person, and the way that he refused to deploy the kind of clichés (both emotional and intellectual) that are almost endemic in British poetry. However much one might have admired the restraint, the sure lineation, the grim precision of the descriptions, the poems were low-wattage. Little seemed at stake in their movements and turns. But towards the end, especially in some of the poems taken from *The Looters* (1989) and *Hey Fatman* (1994), it was clear that something new was happening. Minhinnick's purview was widening to include all kinds of things in strange associations; his imagination was becoming more agile and original. A few years on, *After the Hurricane* delivers manifold on those hints.

What will readers coming to Minhinnick's poetry for the first time encounter? The locales of *After the Hurricane* range from North America to Wales to Iraq (the last frequently). It is a mark of his continued restraint, or discretion, that the reader gets little idea of what his business was in all of these places, Iraq for obvious reasons being particularly intriguing. And yet the experiences and images he relates are intense. One thinks of the difficult ways in which *Briggflatts* can be considered an autobiographical poem, as Bunting himself conceived it. Another important element is a hardboiled tone that is reminiscent of the work of Michael Hofmann and Jamie McKendrick ("It's a quiet night. // Apart from the girls upping the body / Count on a Maximum Karnage video"). He says somewhere here that he has "seen orchids with faces / like cadillacs and pterodactyls", and such skill with metaphor is widespread. The narratives of the book are often punctuated by a mordant, epigrammatic wit, but then just as deftly they will swerve into sumptuous lyricism. Another characteristic feature is the way he masterfully registers how technology has insinuated its way through our bodies and our consciousness (e.g., "Elementary Songs"). In formal terms, he ranges from stanzaic free verse to rhyming couplets; there are many sequences of short takes, as for instance "Twenty-Five Laments for Iraq", which Michael Schmidt pre-emptively included in his anthology, *Twentieth-Century Poetry in English* (1999).

But a list of remarks of this kind will hardly persuade, so here is the last stanza of "Mr Multitude":

> Such swarms.
> Our eyes drank until we turned for home
> to sprawl before *Fargo*'s white farrago
> (those Coen Brothers' videos with a whole shelf to themselves)
> and as we slept
> the deer in the aspen wood
> withdrew their hooves from pockets of silence:
> the deer in the aspen wood
> were a shoal that leapt the electric fence,
> their eyes a meteor shower falling through the dark:
> while over our heads
> the sky's migratory lightnings
> burned and fell out of the north,
> burned and fell and burned again
> though daybreak could come no closer
> than its appointed time.

The "appointed time" of the last line carries overtones of mortality, as the poem is written to a friend who is undergoing a serious, possibly fatal, operation. The poem also tells how the poet and the addressee once drove through a "Hutterite" landscape, possibly the same place where *Fargo*'s grisly action takes place. But of course that's only to remark on some of the echoes which this passage includes. What is also admirable is the delicacy and precision of the descriptions of the fauna, and the way in which it freights emotion without being reduced to mere symbol.

After the Hurricane is 119 pages long, and I can't hope to indicate its force and variety in this review. There were many poems that left me puzzled after repeated readings, but their difficulty was an incitement, adjacent as they were to poems like "Mr Multitude", "The Orchards at Cwm y Gaer", "Samphire", "Songs for the Lugmen", "Neolithic", "After the Hurricane", "The Ghost Orchids of Berdun" and "The Porthcawl Preludes", to name some of the highlights. These steely, complex, moving meditations are not short of amazing. Here is a book that can explain a good deal of the weather of our souls.

Barbed Wine

JAMES KEERY

Trevor Joyce, *With the First Dream of Fire They Hunt the Cold: A Body of Work 1966-2000*
New Writers Press & Shearsman Books, £12.95, ISBN 0907562299
Randolph Healy *Green 532: Poems 1983-2000*
Salt, £8.95, ISBN 1876857447

Verses with a Refrain from a Solicitor's Letter

As when a faded lock of woman's hair shall cause a man to cut his throat in a bedroom at five o'clock in the morning . . .

Dear Sir, I was this morning straight
after the news and forecast
hanging from an old appletree in my garden
a small Japanese bell
when I received through the post your importunate
and quite misguided threats

and in this regard time shall be made of the essence

An injunction, you say. An obstruction,
you say. You've a lot of chat for someone
that's not even clear who he's talking to.
Does this help: not only have I
not erected any obstruction
in the form of a barbed wire fence or otherwise

and in this regard time shall be made of the essence

but I'm attempting today to rest and recover
from the effects of an obstruction in my own passages?
I have, it pains me to have to spit it out, a strangury,
and you've got the wrong man, chief,
I've better blockages to worry about
than the one at the back of some godforsaken hotel in Midleton

and in this regard time shall be made of the essence . . .

I like the way the double-take – the poet hanging from an old apple-tree one moment, but *hanging* . . . *a* . . . *Japanese bell* on it the next – is cued by the epigraph; I like the way the mordant courtesy, through teeth gritted in pain, is sustained through eleven stanzas; but most of all I like the way this extraordinary poem has revealed a new meaning at every reading so far. It's a draft suicide note, an ironic Immortality Ode, a Harrowing of the Hell of Writer's Block, a smack at Ulster sectarianism, a parody of everything from legalese to Celtic myth and a transmutation of intimate anguish into a brilliant work of art.

"Verses …" appeared in *stone floods*, published in 1995 by New Writer's Press, which Trevor Joyce co-founded with Michael Smith in 1967. Joyce published four books in his twenties, culminating in *The Poems of Sweeny Peregrine* (1976), a memorable version of the Gaelic text, *Suibhne Gealt*. Then nothing for nearly twenty years. Since *stone floods*, however, he has been prolific – and it's almost all in this amazing "Body of Work", which opens with "The Poems of Sweeny, Peregrine: A Working of the Corrupt Irish Text". Subject to centuries of pious emendation, this strange "Text" is itself a delirious and corrupt "Body" – a point made, with Celtic nicety, by the interpolation of a comma in the title. Joyce extends the conspiracy "to make corruption of the word outpace that of the flesh", yet his work is Pauline also in its concern with (im)mortality ("this corruptible shall put on incorruption") and strewn with tropes from Revelation, including both "the white horse" and "the white stone" ("Owning").

For the record, Joyce's rendition preceded Heaney's (*Sweeney Astray*, 1983), though Flann O'Brien's preceded both (in *At-Swim-Two-Birds*, 1939). I prefer to explore its inter-relationship with "Verses . . .", for between the texts extends a field of force within which all of Joyce's writing gives intriguing readings. Heaney admits to a sense of identification, but, despite Joyce's misgivings, it is he who shares – or has come to share – the pain and alienation of the deranged Celtic "chief". That cunning colloquialism is one of many direct links, including one as intricate as the *Book of Kells*:

> At this last, Sweeny tumbled from the tree and fell to the **gyves** and shackles of his pursuer.// **Locks** and **fetters** were fitted on him and remained, until at last, through manacle and **spancel**, sense returned.

Compare the satirical invocation of Christ in "Verses . . .":

> . . . scattering from his feet a fine debris
> of **locks**, bolts, **spancels**, cuffs, **gyves**, **fetters**, stocks,
> and other miscellaneous hindrances. . .

The grisly disease of "strangury", in which "urine is passed painfully and in drops", is an allegory of strangulation by another of those "blockages", preventing even painful drops of poetry! Deliverance is assured, as the impedimenta of bourgeois property ("stocks" and shares) and restraint (medieval "stocks") are scattered in a glorious cattle-raid on the thesaurus. I was delighted to learn that a "spancel" is "a short, noosed rope used for fettering the hind legs of a cow during milking"; *OED* cites the *Irish Hudibras* (1669): "That ugly Monaghan *Spanci-all*, / The worst of all the Devils", appropriate to the image of the Redeemer "striding across . . . from some new-harrowed hell". Retrospectively, Joyce identifies with the inspired outcast *and* with his adversary, the scholarly St Ronan.

At the beginning of "Verses . . .", "my bell is mute", in ironic contrast to the objectionable "racket" of Ronan's "handbell", but, by the end, "The bell's transformed" by "a laurel leaf" in poetic victory. Sweeny has "a clenched arse", as if suffering a "strangury", describes himself as "a cave of pain" and drinks the "barbed wine" of sloes. "Verses . . . " closes with a cutting cliché – "I trust this terminates our correspondence, Sir" – but the "correspondence" with "Sweeny" is inexhaustible.

The "calculus that stopped my flow" is one of the uric acid "stones" caused by "strangury" and the mathematics by which Joyce must earn his living as a business analyst. Yet it also crystallises a powerful modernist image of immortality – "the white stone" itself, "calculus Minervae" (as in *The White Stones* by Prynne), and the stone rolled away from the tomb of Christ, who will also, in a mythopoeic fantasy, "allow Eurydice ascend" and "remove . . . North / from the needle". This pointed phrase gives a political twist to Joyce's repudiation of "our friend the illicit / erector of barbed wire barricades", just as Sweeny rants at those who have "thrown up palisades against me" – he was, after all, "A madman of Ulster"! In Orphic rage, Joyce ranges an unholy alliance of terrorists and bourgeois villains – "our Neighbourhood Watch", "the polis" and "this damned notary" – against "The Christ of Revolution and of Poetry" (© the late great David Gascoyne).

Randolph Healy is an engaging postmodernist. I like the way his children increase in number for every new biographical note, I like the exuberant baby daughter on the cover of *Green 532* and I like his entire freedom from the misogynistic Free State modernism of the likes of Devlin and Beckett (who thought *Whoroscope* was a master-wheeze of a title). His great theme is the simultaneous richness and randomness of creation. Here's the ending of the first poem, "Mutability Checkers":

> . . . I dreamed a random river
> whose surface's inflexions shimmered
> with every possible geometry
> where all envisaging blindness hatched
> and crossed as chance, swollen with potential,
> surged against the given, sculpting a world
> where botched and sublime bloomed without design.

And here's an epigram from *Chance and Necessity* by the arch-mechanist of heredity: "a truly blind process can result in anything, even vision". Monod's startling paradox raises "all-envisaging blindness" to a higher power; Healy's lines are imaginatively rich but rhythmically poor, the protean metaphor clogged with tautology. *Arbor Vitae* is an intriguing triptych, but adds up to less than the sum of its parts, or even those of its "Note", which explains all its anagrams, acrostics and Prolog-commands, with a stinging indictment of "Oralism" in deaf-education (one of the poet's daughters is deaf). Many of the 42 anagrams of "(The) Republic of Ireland" are ingeniously apt ("creed liable if up North … in half-policed beer rut"), but I'm not sure . . . If exuberance is beauty, this is a beautiful book, but its author strikes me as the healthy oyster that doesn't have the pearl.

The Flame of Wandering

JONATHAN TREITEL

Yehuda Halevi, *Poems from the Diwan*, translated from the Hebrew by Gabriel Levin
Anvil Press, £9.95, ISBN 0856463337

THE UNIVERSE SHUDDERS and we have slid back 900 years. We are in Granada, in Islamic Andalusia. Abu I-Hassan Ibn Hallewi is reciting:

> Bear arms against the victim of your desire
>> and kindle love with the flame of wandering,
> since you despise me, aim your lance,
>> and as I loathe myself – pierce me through . . .

This is characteristic Sufi poetry – the welcoming of humiliation, the deliberate blurring of the boundary between an erotic declaration to a human lover and to the Divine. Except the poem is not in Arabic but Hebrew, and abounds with allusions not to the Quran but to the Bible. The author – known commonly under his Hebrew name of Yehuda Halevi – was one of the finest poets during what is sometimes called The Golden Age of Islamic Spain. "Golden" is relative. Only by comparison to Christendom was Islamic Spain tolerant. Halevi himself had to flee several times, due to various waves of war and persecution. The civilisation in which he thrived, in which Jews and Christians could learn from Muslims, and to a lesser degree *vice versa*, was fragile, and was soon to be destroyed.

In addition to being a poet, Halevi was a court doctor, a businessman, and a philosopher. His Socratic dialogue, *The Book of Refutation and Proof with Regard to the Humiliated Religion*, affected to prove conclusively that Judaism was superior to the rival monotheisms. Today he is often presented as a proto-Zionist. Israeli schoolchildren sing the following ode of his as a round:

> My heart is in the east and I'm at the far end of the west.
> How can I taste or savour what I eat?
> How keep my vows and pledges – while Zion lies
> shackled to Edom, and I to Arabia bound?
> Giving up the riches of Spain would be as easy for me
> as it were precious in my eyes to feast
> on dust and rubble of the shrine razed to the ground.

As an old man he set out on a haj towards the Holy Land – which he may or may not have reached. One can compare his yearning with that of Arabs in Spain for their ancestral heartland. To quote Abd-ar-Rahman, Emir of Andalusia: "A palm tree I beheld . . . / far in the West, far from the palm-tree land; I said: You, like myself, are far away, in a strange land".

Halevi was skilled at handling Arabic-style verse-forms. Among the most elaborate and fascinating is the muwashshah – a rhymed strophic lyric intended to be sung to music. First a man, using the full range of his courtly rhetoric, is appealing to his beloved:

Graceful doe, pity this heart where you've dwelled.
Know the day you'll leave I'll fall apart.
Even now, as my eyes confront your splendor,
I'm stung by your cheeks' vipers
whose venom burns and drives me away

Astonishingly, the muwashshah ends with a snappy retort from the beloved, and not in formal Hebrew either, but in the Romance-Arabic dialect of the streets: "*Non me tan gas, ya habibi . . .*" – "These breasts, dear, are extra tender – I'm through / with your games. You men are all the same".

Many of Halevi's poems are dedicated to his friends. These sometimes come across as conventionally homoerotic. Mostly they dwell on the absence rather than the presence of the friend:

Even as youngsters we were marked by partings.
The river of weeping flows through the ages,
so why quarrel with time that hasn't sinned,
or days that bear no wrong, fixed
in their heavenly circuits where nothing is bent or twisted?

His melancholy brings to mind Ovid's *Tristia*. In contrast to the Roman, Halevi did not need to be exiled in person to have cause to mourn; enough that his people was.

Gabriel Levin's translation is elegant, and aptly formal, and captures the poet's mood. His introduction is very informative, the footnotes comprehensive. It is entirely reasonable to read this book as a key to understanding a lost culture. But can it also be seen as a source for a culture which persists today? Scarcely so with regard to contemporary literature – Hebrew and Arabic poets look to Europe or America, seldom to each other. In religion there is but a faintly surviving Jewish-Sufi tradition. Yet in the nexus of ideas that contribute to Zionism / post-Zionism / Palestinian nationalism – pride in loss, yearning, eroticisation of the land and of the people, the desire for redemptive degradation – Jews and Arabs continue to influence one another.

Poetic Staples

JEREMY NOEL-TOD

Smith/Doorstop Books (£3)
Sue Wood, *Woman Scouring a Pot*
Chris Considine, *Swaledale Sketchbook*
Jennifer Copley, *Ice*
Annemarie Austin, *Debatable Land*
Thumbscrew Press (£4)
Anne Stevenson, *Hearing with My Fingers*
Andrew McNeillie, *One for the Road*
Peter McDonald, *As If*
Simon Carnell, *Notes of Several Experiments*

PAMPHLETS ARE THE ideal medium for modern poetry. Not as far as the booktrade is concerned: they are palpably cheap to produce, so cannot be marked up much, and, being literally spineless, do not suit the packed shelf. But the contemporary template of thirty-lyrics-and-a-long-one is an often unnaturally imposed standard, in unhappily flatulent competition with the short novel. A pamphlet gives the poet the freedom allowed other artists to determine the exact size of a discrete work. If you have a baker's dozen or so of good poems, why spread them thin, or sit on them? And why pretend the audience for them is much more than a baker's dozen squared?

This is not to say that the reader is urged only to read poetry with staples through it. Most pamphlets are not great art. Although market forces are undeniably philistine and unfair, there are other reasons why some poets find their level at the small press.

It is easy to mouse through Smith/Doorstop's latest pamphlets for samples of what Craig Raine once called "legospeak", the building block clichés of current poetic diction. The marriage of Hughes and Plath is still producing festival-prize-winning daughters, adept at the Big Bad Man poem and the Nice Big Bull poem (sometimes combined). It is a poetry of precise-sounding imprecisions. "There is something fanatical, / too, in its dervish dance", writes Chris Considine, with elegant redundancy, of a Hughesian skylark. Jennifer Copley mistakes obscurely personal associations – "his breath is cold, / colder than camel-bone" – for original similes. And Sue Wood attempts rather desperately to contain the influence of Plath by titling her weakest poem "Sylvia Plath is Reincarnated as a Tulip" ("The bee violates me. It is as randy / as soldiers sexed up on war").

But the well-produced pamphlet has a winning humility which declaws the catty critic. These books are short, neat and cheap. Each has its moments of real talent. Wood's detailed recollection of being a conjuror's assistant (seeing "the trick mirror flash, / the doves' shit liming their air-hole cover"); Considine's lambs at market, "Stars today and meat tomorrow"; Copley's bare observation of bereavement:

> "Give me my mother back", I say
> to the pristine fridge,
> the crumbless table cloth.

A fourth pamphlet in the series is given to a stronger voice. Annemarie Austin's

Debatable Land is a set of poems positioned at various angles around a father with senile dementia. The disjunctive verse accords poignantly with the distress caused by the condition:

> Here is a photograph of someone.
> It's your sister or it's me. And this one
> is my grandmother in her pony trap.
> She's still alive you know. Tell me
> how my grandmother died long ago.

Thumbscrew Press has launched itself with some better known names. The pamphlets are equally neatly produced – although the paper is oddly glossy – but the stakes are higher. The critic feels less kind when presented with middling stuff by a press which began as a magazine that prided itself on upbraiding the mediocre.

Anne Stevenson's is the most venerable reputation on display, but on this showing it is not clear why. *Hearing with my Fingers*, from its title onwards, contains more bad writing than good. One poem, moralising over the Foot and Mouth crisis, states emptily "If myths were mortal, panic would cull the devil". Which rather misses the point about a) myths and b) the devil. Another seems ready-made for inclusion in the inevitable sequel to Bloodaxe's *Staying Alive* anthology (*Keeping It Up*) – a maudlin monologue given to a woman with a wasting disease:

> Don't laugh when I tell you, all I paint is flowers.
> As long as my Minnie Mouse paw can grip the brush
> I forget my melting bones – for those few hours.

"At the Grave of Ezra Pound" muses that "Whatever he might be writing / Wrathfully against our age / Moulders unheard". Unheard, also, is the sound of E.P. revolving like a kebab six feet down.

Craig Raine's "legospeak", back in 1984, included "sunsets" which are invariably "raw". In Andrew McNeillie's *One for the Road* the grand tradition lives on: "winter's red-/ raw sun, the slate-blue wash of sky" ("Chaffinch (Fringilla coelebs)"). Almost all the poems are occasioned by, and named after, a bird; the pamphlet is offered as "a continuation or extension" of the "Plato's Aviary" poems in *Nevermore*, McNeillie's first collection. Some finer pastoral touches corroborate the praise which that book attracted – "the stream's / Glacier fritters briefly in a shallow run / Of stones". Overall, though, the criticism of a sandpiper being immortalised by McNeillie – "Going twee-ee, and again twee-..." – seems not unjust.

If Sylvia Plath owns most of the bricks in the women's lego box, Paul Muldoon now provides the men's. His lilting, quizzical colloquialisms are an insidious influence – see the numerous sentences in McNeillie which turn out to be leisurely questions. Peter McDonald's *As If* is also susceptible to havering Muldoonisms, "as I picked my way, if way you could call / it". In fairness this may be partly attributable to a common project: both Northern Irish poets are investigating what happens when Yeats' grandly rhyming syntax encounters a tougher, cagier idiom. McDonald's is a lean poetic unusually reliant on cumulative force of phrasing. His dry style complements his subject here: the mutual, sterile bitterness of a parting couple. There are some longueurs which go beyond the call of mimesis. But at its best – that is, when not rhyming "close" with "otiose" – there is a finely measured terseness to the lyric footwork reminiscent of the darker poems of Edward Thomas: "the game and I no longer match, / for I can't win, or win much"; "frost may come yet like a knife, / late, and there may be late snow // coming from somewhere even now".

Another tell-tale Muldoon trick is the punning revivification of cliché. McNeillie's "Moorhen" has "All its eggs in one basket"; McDonald fights to save rosebushes which have almost "lost the plot". They have also nearly "given up the ghost"; over in Simon Carnell's *Notes of Several Experiments*, the "Eskimo curlew / gave up the ghost" a long time ago. The revival of cliché now has its own clichés.

Carnell is the newest of the Thumbscrew authors, and one still in danger of losing the plot to Muldoon. "Think of one lit thing and you'll think of another" begins "Lit". That is, if you haven't already thought of Muldoon's "Something Else" ("which made me think / of something else, then something else again"). The poem itself is a clever, attentive piece of writing:

> The dashboard with its full set on
> in motorway fog – including the cobalt one
> with black pictogram showing "full-beam",
> in a square like the lit ones with sliding caps
> you close in arcade bingo when your number is up.

The problem with English imitators of Muldoon is that they lack the volatile subtext of the Troubles to give their mental meanderings his ironic pressure of significance. Carnell's travel poems only relocate the problem. But there is sparky variety, a concise ear and eye, and some ambition here (a Paulinesque poem on the 1930s as "The Heroic Age of Collage"). Even if his first full collection, *Lit*, turns out to be more of the polished same, the pamphlet after that could well be something else again.

Artists' Notes

Conor McGrady (pp. 52–3) was born in Northern Ireland and currently lives in New York. His work has been exhibited internationally, most recently at the Whitney Museum, NY: "All the paintings and drawings that I produce are based on either first-hand experience or oral histories of encounters with violence. In the past year I have focused on producing an extended body of works on paper that carry the ideas in the paintings further and expand on them. In these drawings I use an economical or distilled line to explore the impact of military control on domestic and public space, and the latent residue of trauma inherent in seemingly innocuous objects and places. In these drawings, violence becomes a form of omission pertaining to a removal of self-worth or dignity, and the empty spaces that permeate the drawings are intended to resonate a sense of disquiet or unease. While drawing on my experiences of Northern Ireland, the aim of these works is to provide a space shaped by contemporary social experience in any context, and to open that space for questions, discussion and criticism."

Emma Byrne (pp. 81–4) lives and works in Ireland: "My work is based on landscape, primarily the landscape which surrounded me as I grew up, a landscape lush and wild and full of secrets. It is a landscape where the past is written in a language of ruins and abandoned houses, of stones and forests. It is a landscape rich in physical beauty, yet it is a landscape where dark and terrible events have occurred, where violence has burned deep marks into the psyche of its inhabitants. It is a mirror which contains all the joy and sadness, the horror and the beauty, that makes us what we are . . . In my work I wish to create visual analogies of this intense experiencing of landscape . . . The works do not aim to be descriptive or straightforwardly expressive, but rather recreate in the mind of the viewer the resonance which attracted me to it in the first place."

Dawn Wood (pp. 102–3) is a poet, painter and science lecturer. She is currently researching ethical aspects of animal husbandry at the University of Abertay, Dundee.

The Questionnaire

Poetry Review invited a number of poets to reply to the question: "Which poet or poets, have you been most surprised to enjoy?" Here we print a selection of responses.

MICHAEL DONAGHY

Personification: no ideas but with wings. Long before Wordsworth rejected it as a contraption of poetic diction, Pope lampooned the Augustan version with the toast "Set Bacchus from his glassy prison free". But remember, in the cult of Dionysus god and wine were indistinguishable in *Theoinus*, the "god-wine" – In Haiti, according to experimental filmmaker and voodoo priestess Maya Deren, death is not a dying man or a corpse. It's the shadowy Baron Ghede de la Croix sporting his top hat and broken sunglasses. Lately, I've been interested in poems where personification lies somewhere between ironic trope and supernatural encounter. I've been hunting the *Melancholy*.

Look at Dürer's sulky angel bored with her educational toys. Looks like she's waiting for someone. Not Milton, though. He seeks "divinest Melancholy // Whose saintly visage is too bright / To hit the sense of human sight" whom he asks to "Dissolve (him) into ecstasies" Not Marvell either. He's pursuing something far more intense: "Magnanimous Despair alone / Could show me so divine a thing, / Where feeble Hope could ne'er have flown, / But vainly flapped its tinsel wing". And certainly not Keats. Who'd mistake this glum creature for his terrifying veiled goddess lying in wait in her dark sanctum deep within the temple of Delight, surrounded by the cloudy souls of those hunters who've burst joy's grape against their palettes and tasted the sadness of her might? Me neither.

Was Keats Japanese? Japanese tourists at his Hampstead shrine might suspect he knew something of *mono no aware*, that exquisite sadness induced by the sight of clouds passing in the sky, by the cherry blossom that blooms for three days before scattering. The Heian master Kukai taught that only such fragile mortal beauty can reveal the Buddha's truth: all that lives must suffer and die. See Paz: *Tres Momentos de la Literatura Japonesa* . . . That's Octavio Paz, who translated Basho and maintained that Lorca absorbed this appetite from haiku . . . That's F. Garcia Lorca, who warned that the *Duende* is neither Muse nor Angel.

These are important distinctions. Dürer's mopey soul is an impostor. She's *Depression* or some minor spirit suffering from that complaint, a condition which drains significance from the world. Its polar (as in bipolar) opposite is that surfeit of meaning which feeds *Melancholy* – or, as anyone who's dined in the company of poets will attest, her hideous bat-winged sister *Paranoia*.

CHARLES TOMLINSON

"Which poet or poets, have you been most surprised to enjoy?" The wording of the invitation to participate in *Poetry Review*'s questionnaire was for me startlingly exact. I was "surprised to enjoy" precisely those poets no one told me about at university – Marlowe, in his versions of Ovid's elegies, for example, and later and more decisively, Dryden's massive selection of Greek and Latin poetry. As I discovered with surprise and delight, his version of the first book of *The Iliad* opened a vista into Homer (no one had pointed out Pope's greatest work, as Doctor Johnson thought it, the complete *Iliad*). Dryden's *Aeneid* (which prompted that undertaking of Pope's) still remains one of the forgotten masterpieces of seventeenth-century poetry. I was surprised to find gradually and increasingly I was becoming a fan of Dryden the translator, but it was many years before I was converted to the idea that the translations contained his best work. The revelation came to me with the translation of Ovid's *Metamorphoses* Dryden had begun to edit and in part translate himself. This was left incomplete at his death and finally appeared in 1717. The younger poets who contributed so brilliantly to this (Pope was one of them) had clearly learned to write by reading Dryden, with his "long majestick march and energy divine". My own initial surprise led to my editing *The Oxford Book of Verse in English Translation*, which demonstrated just how much of our poetry came via translation. This fact really calls for the re-writing of the whole history of English poetry. An awareness of the international scene is valuable to a poet, as I found when translating Antonio Machado and César Vallejo besides Octavio Paz who via translation (we translated each other) became a friend for life. Furthermore Machado taught me to do things no English poetry had brought my way. Paz influenced me to write on political themes and my own poem, "Assassin", drew from him two of his finest essays, both on the psychology of the assassin. Another poet and friend was the Italian Attilio Bertolucci who showed how the domestic scene might enter into poetry. Dryden, as translator, was in many ways the instigator of this unforeseen development in my own work: translation of poetry is, if it is any good, first and foremost poetry.

SUSAN WHEELER

Being surprised to like a poet presupposes an expectation of dislike, naturally, and I have always been an optimistic reader to a fault. But there have been a few cases in which the lore surrounding a poet disinclined me from the get-go. One of these was Sylvia Plath; for a while, when I was a teenager, every literate adult seemed to follow up their initial, "What's your favorite subject?" with "You must read Sylvia Plath!" Granted, the contemporary canon was not a happy lot – Lowell, Berryman, Plath – but that she and Anne Sexton, both suicides, were to be the models for my gender drove me, fittingly, nuts. It took many years for me to read her poems without aversion, and then I was astonished by them.

Later, at Bennington College where I was an awkward undergraduate, the local lore was thick surrounding the poet Howard Nemerov and his legendary poker game with Stanley Edgar Hyman, Paul Feeley, Kenneth Noland – and Bernard Malamud, who was still there. In my mind, I associated this with what I thought of as downmarket posing on the part of the Benningtonians who scared me. That, and tripping lines such as "Your daughter's the cause of this & that erection", encouraged my thinking of his work as macho bluster.

It wasn't until several years later, assigned a review by the *Chicago Tribune*, that I finally read much of his work. Idea-driven, the poems use quick, dry images: "Wolves at the Zoo" "are like big dogs badly drawn, drawn wrong." The "refined feathers" of "bearded goldfish" are "like light in gin". Often wielding pronouncements, Nemerov, like Larkin and Frost, also mocked this authority – obliquely or, as in his barbed "On Being Asked for a Peace Poem," outright – and gave epigrams a dark turn: a "good marriage" means "One should be watching while the other dies"; poets who move from "epigram to epic" as they mature "start out Emily and wind up Walt". The longer meditations, the chilling poems about poetry, the precise perversion of his formal attention – won me over.

ANDREW DUNCAN

Big Wall! Mega Ceiling!

The Turner Prize Exhibition 2002; Tate Modern, London

AS YOU OPEN this magazine – this exhibition will have closed.

On lurching into the exhibition, we are confronted with a wall of 39 paintings by Keith Tyson which looks exactly like the Picture Wall in a primary school classroom. I was swept away by this three-dimensional deluge of colour and dynamics. "The Edges of Things no.29: A Molten Purple Tessellation" shows pseudo-crystalline aquaplaning panes of swirling purple, swelling like the layers of a bulb, shifted like a Dairy Milk wrapper scrumpled after passionate ingestion. "A picture restorer accidentally removes a layer of paint revealing the face of god" is purple drip forms on an ochre background, with purple frottage looking like wood grain. The computer-game screen designs like "Hand-Held Chinese Portal" flash us back to pin-ball tables, wondrous creations of flashing lights, fairground-garish paintings, and silvered metal ballistics. A painted cinema front canopy gives us 30-40 enticing film precis (or a precis of 1 film?) including "mermaids gossiping about last tide's sexual exploits . . . the questionable wisdom of the desert hermit . . . a bust of Thatcher fashioned from Semtex . . . an exact replica of Sacramento . . . madness infecting a ship adrift in the doldrums . . . Tesla's Third Eye blinking . . . a red brick galleon sinks swiftly". Tyson has a mighty conceptual imagination which is equally fluent with words or images. A Table Top Tale called "Anticipating a tumbling coin from the cherubic mint" eluded my understanding, but was dreamlike, enchanting, funny, and involved a lion plugged into a toaster. Tyson's pictures are really cutaway illustrations of machines he has designed but hasn't got around to building. Not only is the wonderful large- and small-scale variety of his pictures an illustration of information and probability as factors affecting the original design of the brain and its immediate, transient, states, but also he can think about thermodynamics. I think maybe the reason I was so thrilled by Tyson's exhibition is that I flashed back to my childhood – which had a lot to do with Loughborough University of Technology, and with engineering. Tyson did a degree in Mechanical Engineering, and this is why his work is filled with fit structures, so world-embodying that they seem kinetic even when they're static. I slipped back to a childhood of techno-optimism about a future which corrupt Southerners stole from us. And to a 1960s full of shiny surfaces, self-acting machines, mind-expanding transformations. He did remind me of 1960s artists like Tom Phillips and Öyvind Fahlström, but even more of Thomas Pynchon. Tyson was shortlisted in recognition of *three* exhibitions in the last twelve months – this guy is toast. He also did a "BA in Alternative Practice" at the University of Brighton. Wow! how cool is that!

Liam Gillick shows "Coats of Asbestos Spangled with Mica", which is a ceiling of perspex panels with a kind of fly-tower made of aluminium strips installed above it. As you walk around the room, the perspex tiles modulate the visible colour of the aluminium members. The space above holds apparent catwalks of a city aloft, a self-exfoliating structure. Our eye

---

This review was received before the announcement that Keith Tyson had won the 2002 Turner Prize.

moves in an environment of colours – height becomes walkable, in a symbolic reconstruction of the home of the primate cortex – coloured fruit and branches of trees offering paths. This simple structure, based on transparency and right-angles, takes on the permanent roof structure above, turning a dozen yards of vertical recession into apparent reflection, peaking with the mighty four-blade propeller structure of the naked roof web, with their fishbone struts running off to either side. My notes say "half crystallographer, half typographer". However cerebral this proof in the geometrical sublime seems, the colour contrasts (blue . . . orange) are mood-shifting and speak to the reptile brain. Keywords: *aluminium lierne; visible carcass of stresses; labyrinthine clarity; the imaginary in geometry; generatable space.*

The project reminds me of the aluminium rounds, blocks, and cylinders which Terence Gray used at the Festival Theatre, Barnwell, to build constructivist stage sets, with colour provided by projection from a bank of lights (the most advanced in Europe in 1928). The aluminium offers highly reflective, non-glare, colourless blanks suffusable by beams of pure colour. The concept of a spatial, unfigured, volume dramatised by selective lighting reminds me of the caves of Les Eyzies, as described by Annette Laming, the magical recesses of the earth revealed by initiatory torchlight.

The catalogue tells us that the layout of the tiles is based on the 9x9 grid which was the modulus for the architects designing the Tate Extension in 1979 – it's almost the building speaking its own structure via LED. The catalogue also refers us to a 1905 novel by Jean Tarde called *Underground Man*, which I checked out in the British Library. In AD 2489, the sun fails, changing colour several times, and the remnants of mankind move underground to live off geothermal energy. The tints of the ceiling panels refer, I suppose, to the autumnal decline of the sun. This society is post-economic and its members dedicate themselves exclusively to artistic pleasure and subtle intellectual questions. This setting redefines the Tate as a grotto or crypta, its roof as a cladding hiding millions of tons of living rock – and us as these virtuoso exquisites, enjoying haughty delights which are disguised as the Tate's British Collection. In this mineral realm, the asbestos and mica are what the women's robes are made of. And then we are told of "metallic iridescence with its infinite tints": this must have been my fellow visitors – we were, after all, *inside* the work.

Some of the ambient bleating has alluded to "conceptual bullshit". This charge requires a response. So, to start with, the concept of a dramatic volume revealed and inspired by light alludes to the painted caves, the cathedrals, and the post-mediaeval theatre – at least. And then there is the fact that several cwt. of square-profile anodised aluminium laths are not dematerialised. It's not about conceptual art, it's about using new media and interoperability. All four artists do use motifs, drawn from Conceptualism. Fluency with words – another common characteristic – may be a return to the whole human being creating whole things.

Minister Kim went on the *Today* programme saying that he rejected this "conceptual art" because he was a socialist. It had never even occurred to me that anyone could look at art which rejects objects, rejects property, and votes rule-free rule-making consciousness into power, dissolving into free interplay across a group of people, and *not* see it as socialist. You dag! Do you think the 1970s were just chapter one of proto-Blairism? Do you really think that achieving freedom from history and breaking out into conceptual thought are separate and distinct processes?

Catherine Yass shows two films of London buildings shot from an unmanned surveillance helicopter and a Cessna light plane. The eye as shooting star, the eye as wind. Film and aircraft – the Howard Hughes franchise. They reminded me of a 1950 documentary called *River of Time*, with a wonderful aerial tracking shot along the eleven miles of docklands as it was then. The idea is to capture the soaring and plummeting of dream flights. *Mary Poppins*, with its swoops over London roofscapes, is also a reference point. The rendition of dream flight obviously appeals to almost everyone, so the questions here are mainly about technique. Yass mixes patrimonial ideas with technical ineptitude and fear of making decisions. Keywords: *techno-autism; no, I didn't edit; gee, system-built buildings are like Status Quo concerts; travel sickness; halation; wilful blankness; The Lost Patrol; the focus-puller was on lunch-break.* I understand from reviews that these works shown are not representative of Yass at her best, or of the exhibition she was shortlisted for.

Fiona Banner offers us a handwritten, blow-by-blow record of a porn film called *Arsewoman in Wonderland*. Her works are like her name. And the title reveals the plot. One of the long-standing conventions of the art world is that someone who catastrophically fails to make words do their bidding is always described as "exploring the possibilities of language". Banner is quite cheerful and uses an attractive red colour, and is good at writing in straight lines. The failure to credit the original scriptwriter is unethical. Keywords: *the Murray Walker of porn; kittenish shittiness of concetto; wilful blankness; literalism in ever so bold red lettering; no, I don't edit; simulation of consciousness; copy of subjectivity; blow-up petulant bletherskite artiste figurine; well, you needn't.*

Editorial Note

Politics surface in this issue of *Poetry Review*. In her discussion of Peter Robinson's *Poetry, Poets, Readers*, Andrea Brady asks how poetry can relate to the institutions of public life. Andrew Duncan answers the question, in one way at least, by having an argument with a politician. Can it be right, he wonders in his review of the Turner Prize exhibition, that, as Kim Howells asserted, conceptual art is not socialist? Or might it not be the case that art which "rejects property, and votes rule-free rule-making consciousness into power" has, in fact, more to do with socialism than does a Blairite government? Reviewing Yehuda Halevi, Jonathan Treitel reads Halevi's poetry in the light of "the ideas that contribute to Zionism/post-Zionism/Palestinian nationalism", optimistically observing that, in their poetic traditions at least, "Jews and Arabs continue to influence each other". And, reflecting on a different national crisis, Edna Longley insists that the linguistic self-awareness which characterises Paul Muldoon's poetry should be read not as a kind of abstract playfulness, but as a poetic response to the volatile facts of recent Northern Irish history. Needless to say, these writers do not share a politics. What they do share, however, and what the various apprehensions of The *Poetry Review* Essay amplify, is a sense that poets can and will participate in the arguments that shape collective life.

Geoffrey Dearmer Prize

We are delighted to announce that the winner of the Geoffrey Dearmer poetry prize 2002 is David Gravender, for his poem "Uht-Sang", which was published in *Poetry Review* 92/3 (Autumn 2002). Gravender's star is clearly in the ascendant as he has just been awarded a Poetry Fellowship by the National Endowment for the Arts for 2003–2004.

The judge for the Geoffrey Dearmer prize was the poet Stephen Knight, who said: "I wanted to be affronted, to admonish the poets for taking liberties; to feel superannuated, in other words. It was a strong shortlist, with all but one of the names new to me. Simon Carnell has been around for a while. His 'Red Earth Dreaming' is a characteristically curious aggregation. It's good to hear he has a book forthcoming. I was also taken by the odd angles of Anthony Caleshu's three poems: 'I had to be rescued by a pretty lifeguard who later told me / about the prescription protection her dermatologist prescribed'. Veronica Gaylie's 'Prayers' is a gem. Who'd have thought a poem that ropes in the Rolling Stones's drummer could be not only amusing but affecting. Evan Rail's 'And Counting' announces, with bracing confidence, 'No one can stop me today, not tonight'. His poem's sweeping assertions and abnormal confidence certainly made me feel old. In the end, I went for David Gravender because I'm a sucker for good American free-verse. He has an easy manner, youthful poise, daring. The noirish moments of 'Uht-Sang' are entirely beguiling – 'Dead slumber after three days driving' is a terrific opener – and its atmospheres are vivid: the finger of chill, the fogs of blood and skin, and the fragrant breeze. How does he get away with 'the spirits of the lost – slain or ignored'? Or the final image of an iceberg 'real as spirit, fathomless'? I don't know, but I'm very glad that he does."

David Gravender says: "Attention and recognition that an award like the Geoffrey Dearmer Prize brings are, if not essential to a poet's work, very welcome attendants. They are like an amplification system for the small voice crying in the wilderness that a new poet's work is. They give the poems a momentarily louder voice, and let the poet know in turn that the poems are being registered. I'm therefore very grateful and excited for this opportunity of recognition, to be heard, and hope it brings my manuscript *Field of Vision* to a few more ears and eyes."

Now in its fifth year, the Geoffrey Dearmer Prize was set up with a generous bequest to honour the noted First World War poet, and the Poetry Society's oldest member, Geoffrey Dearmer. By establishing an endowment fund, the Dearmer family have enabled the Poetry Society to award an annual prize to the *Poetry Review* "new poet of the year" who has not yet published a book.